Low-Fat, No-Fat
Asian Cooking

Low-Fat, No-Fat Asian Cooking

150 Simple, Delicious Recipes for a Healthier You

Reader's
Digest

The Reader's Digest Association, Inc.
New York, New York / Montreal

Contents

Asian cooking – the low-fat way!

At the heart of Asian cooking is the balance of tastes – sweet, sour, salty and spicy – and use of the freshest possible ingredients. Many Asian meals are naturally low in fat, consisting of only a small amount of protein, such as meat or tofu, with a large serve of vegetables, and flavoured with herbs and spices. These are either cooked quickly over high heat in a steamer or wok to retain texture and colour, or braised or stewed slowly in a hotpot to develop layers of fragrance and flavour.

In creating this book, we have selected low-fat recipes from cuisines across the region – from China and Japan in the north, travelling south to Vietnam, Thailand, Malaysia and Singapore. While each country boasts its own unique blend of flavours and styles, Asian dishes are almost always shared at the table and served with either rice or noodles. You will discover a world of beautifully fresh, healthy food, from traditional favourites such as wonton noodle soup and sweet-and-sour pork to modern classics such as Thai fish cakes and Singapore noodles, plus many more.

The recipes in this book contain no more than 30 g total fat (8 g saturated fat) per serving. No optional ingredients, serving suggestions or garnishes have been included in the nutritional analysis for each recipe.

Once you have purchased a few basic Asian ingredients, and stocked up some of the essential flavourings and condiments (see pages 10–15), you will be surprised at how simple and nutritious it is to create these truly versatile and impressive low-fat Asian dishes.

THE EDITORS

Understanding low-fat cooking

Asian food has a reputation for being one of the most healthy cuisines in the world, as well as providing a wonderful spectrum of unique tastes and unforgettable blending of flavours.

The Asian diet

The healthy Asian diet is characteristically low in both saturated fat and total fat. Daily meals are based on abundant plant foods rather than animal foods, with emphasis on freshness and unique blends of herbs, spices and sauces to maximise flavour. The key to a healthy diet is to eat a wide variety of foods, to maintain the proportion of the kilojoules or calories you get from fat at around 30 per cent or less of your total kilojoule (calorie) intake, and to keep saturated fats to a minimum.

What is fat?

All oils are pure fat but are an essential part of a healthy diet. Most health experts recommend reducing consumption of saturated fats and **trans** fats (mainly from animals) and replacing them where possible with either monounsaturated or polyunsaturated fats (mainly from plants, nuts and seeds).

Omega-3

One class of polyunsaturated fatty acids are the Omega-3 fatty acids. These are essential for good health as they can't be manufactured by the body alone. Fish oils and oily fish, such as salmon, mackerel, sardines and tuna, are all rich sources of Omega-3 fatty acids and often appear in Asian dishes.

Glycaemic index (GI)

By including good essential fatty acids in your meals, you can slow the rate at which a meal is digested, or absorbed, into the bloodstream. This, in turn, lowers the GI of the overall meal, making you feel full for longer and making it much better for a healthy diet.

Darker oils, such as toasted sesame oil, have stronger flavours, so use in small quantities as a flavour enhancer during or at the end of cooking, rather than as a cooking oil.

Which oil for cooking?

Some oils are more useful than others for healthy cooking or flavouring. All fats will burn if heated high enough, but the smoke point for each oil (that is, when the oil starts to smoke and burn) is different depending on its chemical composition. Most highly refined oils have higher smoke points. Cooking oils with a high smoke point are especially suited to stir-fries and high heat cooking, but can still be used in salad dressings and marinades.

Types of oils and fats

Use strongly flavoured oils sparingly and milder oils for general cooking as they add very little flavour to the dish. **CANOLA**, corn, rice bran, peanut, soybean and safflower oil all have high smoke points, are rich in monounsaturated or polyunsaturated fats, and most have a mild flavour, making them perfect for stir-frying.

COCONUT CREAM can be used instead of oil to sauté or stir-fry. It enhances the coconut flavour, but is also high in saturated fat so should be used sparingly. You can substitute it with low-fat coconut cream.

SESAME OIL can burn at low temperatures so is best used to enhance flavours of other cooking oils, salad dressings or for sprinkling over stir-fries.

VEGETABLE OIL is made up of a blend of different oils that can have different smoke points and flavours. As the blend is not usually specified, opt instead for a specific oil for cooking.

GHEE is a clarified butter used in Indian cooking. It has been heated previously and milk solids removed, so it can be heated to higher temperatures without burning.

COOKING OIL SPRAYS are also useful for low-fat cooking as they add an insignificant amount of fat to a recipe, but still prevent foods from sticking to pans and help promote the browning of foods.

Storing oils

Oils can become rancid when exposed to heat, air and light so it is important to store them in an airtight container with as little 'air space' between the oil and the container as possible. Keep in a dark cupboard or in the refrigerator; it may go cloudy when chilled but will clear when it comes back to room temperature.

How to reduce fat content

- Use lean cuts of meat and trim any excess fat. Remove any skin from chicken.
- Although nuts are naturally high in good oils, use sparingly to reduce fat content.
- Many Asian dishes include coconut cream and/or coconut milk, which are both high in saturated fats. Use sparingly or substitute with low-fat coconut milk. Alternatively, use evaporated milk and coconut essence. In some recipes, Greek-style yogurt could also be substituted but do not allow it to boil or it may curdle and split.
- Change the cooking method; for example, steam vegetables rather than pan-fry them.
- For stir-fries, use a non-stick pan with oil spray instead of pouring oil.
- Baste or oil the meat directly instead of pouring lots of oil into the pan – this will ensure you are only using as much oil as you need to cook the meat.
- Wrap food in banana leaves or baking paper so no oil is required during cooking.

No fat is needed for food cooked in parcels.

Asian ingredients

Asian cooking is a balance of flavours, textures and colours. Using the freshest produce available with some basic Asian ingredients will ensure the sweet, sour, salty, hot and spicy balance in each dish is easily achievable and tastes terrific.

Rice, wrappers and noodles

There are many varieties of rice, wrappers and noodles that are used in specific Asian countries, each suited to certain dishes. Here is a guide to some of the most common varieties used in Asian cooking.

Rice varieties

There is an amazing array of rice types to choose from to suit both savoury and sweet dishes. Here are a few.

BASMATI Long-grain rice with an aromatic flavour especially suited to Indian dishes.

BROWN A nutritious rice variety, as the bran layer is left on. It takes longer to cook than white rice but soaking rice overnight will reduce the cooking time. It is sold in both short- and long-grain varieties.

GLUTINOUS A sticky rice that is commonly used in Asian desserts and sweets.

JASMINE A soft, fragrant rice suited to serving alongside most Asian dishes. Also known as Thai fragrant rice.

Short- and long-grain rice

Short-grain rice is a moist rice, which means it requires less liquid when cooking. The stickiness of cooked rice makes it ideal to eat with chopsticks because the grains cling together. Long-grain is drier and requires more liquid when cooking. The cooked grains remain quite firm and separate, making them less suitable to eat with chopsticks.

SUSHI Short- or medium-grain rice, also sold as 'sushi rice'. Once cooked it becomes sticky, so it holds together well, making it perfect for making sushi.

WILD RICE Not a true rice, wild rice has a nutty flavour and chewy texture. Wash thoroughly before cooking. It is more expensive than many other rice varieties so is often used in combination with short- or long-grain rices.

Wrapper varieties

Wrappers are available from most supermarkets. Won ton and rice paper varieties are used in many recipes.

RICE PAPER Often used in Thai and Vietnamese cooking, it comes in various sizes and is available dried. Soften in warm water briefly before using.

WON TON (GOW GEE) Available in squares or rounds, these paper-thin wrappers come in various sizes.

Wild rice   *Basmati rice*   *Won ton wrappers*

Noodle varieties

There are many varieties, shapes and colours of noodles, available both dried and wok-ready, or fresh, from the refrigerated section of Asian grocery stores and some supermarkets. As a general rule, yellow noodles are made from wheat flour, water and sometimes egg, and white noodles are made from either rice or wheat. Preparation is different but in most recipes the type of noodles can be substituted.

Tip As soon as noodles are cooked, rinse under running water to stop the cooking process. If not using immediately, toss with a little oil to prevent them from sticking together.

BUCKWHEAT These include soba noodles (Japanese buckwheat noodles) and are made from buckwheat or a mixture of buckwheat and wheat flour. They are sold wok-ready (fresh) or dried, and are used in salads, soups and stir-fries.

CELLOPHANE Most commonly made from mung bean flour, these noodles are transparent once cooked. Also known as Chinese vermicelli, they are commonly used in salads, soups and rice paper rolls. You can also deep-fry dried noodles until they puff up and use as a garnish.

EGG These noodles are usually made from wheat flour, salt, water and eggs and are yellow in colour and include the popular hokkien noodle. They are sold dried or wok-ready in refrigerated packets from most supermarkets. Use egg noodles in stir-fries, soups and salads. To prepare fresh egg noodles, cover briefly with hot water, then drain to remove the oil and separate the noodles. Toss quickly to cook, being careful not to overcook or they can become mushy. To prepare dried noodles, simmer in boiling water following the packet instructions, before draining and using as directed.

RICE Made from rice flour, there are many types available in various sizes, sold dried and wok-ready. Fresh noodles are sold in folded sheets that can be cut to preferred thickness. Microwave, steam or submerge briefly in warm water to separate the noodles. Add at the end of cooking in stir-fries, soups and salads. Dried noodles are available in packets in various thicknesses. Rice vermicelli noodles are very thin, rice stick noodles are thicker, and fine rice noodles are in between. All need to be soaked in hot water to soften before using.

WHEAT Made from wheat, these noodles can be dried in flat, long thin strands or sold fresh. They are often used in soups and stir-fries, are white in colour and include udon and somen noodles, both popular in Japanese soups. Can also be eaten chilled.

COLOURED AND FLAVOURED NOODLES Generally the colour of the noodles is a result of the flavouring agent used in making them.

Cream (natural) – somen (thin noodles); udon (thick)
Green (spinach) – spinach noodles; cha soba (green tea buckwheat noodles)
Brown (buckwheat) – soba
Yellow (egg) – hokkien; ramen; fried, ready-to-use, crunchy yellow egg noodles.

Cellophane noodles   *Buckwheat noodles*   *Rice noodles*

Flavourings and condiments

One of the most distinctive things about Asian food is the wonderful variety of sauces that can enliven fresh produce. Depending on the country of origin, the use of basic fresh spices can also vary the taste of a dish – simply using the right amount at the right time can impart unique and bold flavours to the most simple of dishes.

Chillies

As a general rule the smaller the chilli the hotter the flavour. Red chillies have completely ripened so have a slightly sweeter flavour than green peppery chillies. Reduce chilli heat by scraping out the seeds and white pith with a teaspoon.

Chillies

Galangal

Coconut milk and cream

Canned coconut cream is thicker and creamier than coconut milk. Low-fat coconut cream has 50 per cent less fat. Once opened, transfer the contents of the can to an airtight container and refrigerate for up to 3 days or freeze for up to 3 months.

Tip Before buying, shake the can to determine the thickness of coconut milk. Usually, the thicker the better. After opening the can, scoop off the cream and use instead of oil for cooking.

Fish sauce

Used to season and enhance flavours. Some brands are quite fishy and/or salty, so taste before adding to a dish.

Galangal

This spicy aromatic rhizome has a distinct ginger flavour. It is often added to soups and curry pastes. Peel with a sharp knife and chop before pounding with a mortar and pestle or spice grinder.

Garlic

Choose firm bulbs with no soft or discoloured blemishes. Store in a cool, dry place.

Garlic

Kaffir limes

Ginger

Peel and finely chop or grate before using. Ginger with firm, shiny skin is younger ginger and will have a fresher, less pronounced taste. Older ginger has a stronger, peppery taste and a more fibrous texture.

Tip Freeze old-season ginger and grate it while still frozen, to break up the fibrous texture. If using firm young ginger, you do not need to peel it first, just wipe and grate it with the skin on.

Lemongrass

Palm sugar

Tamarind

Wasabi

Kaffir limes (makrut)

Both the leaves and zest of this dark green bumpy-skinned fruit are used in curries, soups and salads. Although not the same flavour, substitute grated lime zest if kaffir limes are not available.

Lemongrass

Use the white, bottom third of the stem. Discard green tops and any tough outer layers. Finely chop or bruise the stem with the handle of a large knife to release the flavours.

Tip Add discarded lemongrass tops to boiling water when steaming or scatter over the base of the steamer to infuse a subtle flavour.

Palm sugar (jaggery)

Made from the sap of palm trees. Light brown to black in colour, it is usually sold in hard cakes. The darker the colour the stronger the caramel flavour. Substitute with soft brown sugar if unavailable.

Vinegars

RICE VINEGAR Mildest of the vinegars with subtle flavour.
SUSHI VINEGAR Made from rice vinegar, sugar and salt, it is used in sushi rice; it also makes excellent no-oil salad dressings.

Rice wines

Used for cooking only. Sake (Japanese rice wine) and shaoxing rice wine from China are the most popular. Mirin is also a sweeter version that is used in Japanese sauces and glazes.

Soy sauce

Chinese light soy sauce is lighter in flavour and colour than dark and is equivalent to shoyu (Japanese soy sauce). Salt-reduced soy sauce is also available.

Sichuan peppercorn

Subtle lemon peppery flavoured spice, used either whole in soups and hotpots or ground into a fine powder.

Tamarind

Sour brown fruit pulp; adds tartness to dishes. It is available as a concentrated pulp or as a paste.

Wasabi

Japanese green horseradish paste made from the wasabi root. Served with sushi and sashimi, it has a distinctly intense flavour and should be used sparingly, or let guests add their own to taste.

Snake beans

Shiitake mushrooms

Daikon

Water chestnuts

Vegetables and fruit

Asian cooking includes an abundance of fresh vegetables and fruits, essential for a low-fat diet. Where you can, buy what is in season and try to make sure it is as fresh as possible as this will make all the difference to flavour.

Asian greens

Bok choy (pak choy), choy sum, gai larn (Chinese broccoli) and wombok (Chinese cabbage) are interchangeable in most stir-fry, hotpot and soup recipes. To keep valuable nutrients, steam the greens or add at the end of cooking.

Bamboo shoots

Mostly used in Chinese and South East Asian cooking, the immature shoots of the bamboo are available in cans from most large supermarkets. Drain before using.

Capsicums (bell peppers)

Many colours from red, green, yellow to purple are now available. Buy glossy fruit, heavy for their size, without blemishes. Eat raw or cooked. Ripe red and yellow capsicums are sweeter and less pungent than the immature green. Banana chillies are similar in flavour to capsicum; eat raw or cooked.

Daikon (long white radish)

Buy firm, unblemished and small vegetables for a slightly sweet, fresh flavour. Peel, dice or slice daikon for stir-fries, hotpots or soups. To eat raw with sashimi or salads, first grate, then soak in cold water for 10 minutes and drain for a crisper texture.

Eggplant (aubergine)

Only large eggplants need to be diced/sliced, sprinkled with salt, left for 30 minutes and rinsed before use to extract bitter juices. Small round apple or finger-shaped Lebanese eggplants can be used as is and have a delicious flavour.

Green papaya and green mango

Green papaya (pawpaw) is slightly sour, although some varieties are sweeter than others. They are used in savoury Thai salads, pickles and chutneys. Once ripe, the orange flesh is sweet. Papaya contains an enzyme, papain, that can be used to tenderise meat, octopus and squid. Green mangoes are a typical addition to summery Asian salads, especially with seafood.

Onions

There is often confusion about different onion varieties. The terms can vary between countries, regions and even stores. In most recipes they can be used interchangeably.

SCALLIONS

Scallions have a mild onion flavour and can be eaten raw or cooked. Scallions have very thin white bases no wider than their long, straight green stems. A green onion or bunching onion has gained the hint of a bulb with maturity; a scallion has not. However, in some countries the scallion may be called a green onion or a green shallot.

GREEN ONIONS

Also known as bunching onions, green onions have long, green, delicate stems and small, very slender, white bulbs.

SPRING ONIONS

An immature onion with a small white bulb and green tops. Spring onions have slightly rounded bulbs that are more defined and a bit larger than the more slender green onions.

FRENCH SHALLOTS

French shallots (eschalots) are small clusters of sweet, mild-flavoured onions that are brown in colour. Asian shallots are a similar size but are purple or red in colour. You can substitute 2 Asian shallots with 1 small red onion if unavailable.

Scallions

Green onions

Spring onions

French shallots

Mushrooms

Fresh button, field, oyster, Swiss brown, shiitake, shimeji, enoki, black and white fungi are all commonly available and have their own unique flavours. Avoid buying any slimy or shrivelled mushrooms. Don't wash mushrooms, just wipe with a damp cloth before eating raw or cooking. Dried mushrooms have a more concentrated flavour than fresh.

Tip If using dried mushrooms, soak them first in warm water for about 20–30 minutes to soften, then remove the hard stems and use the caps as directed. The mushroom soaking liquid can be added to soups and hotpots for additional flavour.

Snake beans (Chinese beans)

Very long green beans used much like any other green beans. Green beans can be used if unavailable.

Snow peas (mangetout)

Buy firm, bright green, unblemished pods. Trim them by snipping off each end and pulling down from one end to remove the 'string'.

Sprouts

Snow pea, daikon, mung bean or bean sprouts add crunch to stir-fries, soups and salads. Buy crisp sprouts, avoiding any with brown tips. Use as soon as possible.

Water chestnuts

Used in Chinese and Thai cooking, water chestnuts are sold in cans and can be eaten raw or cooked.

Wombok (Chinese cabbage)

Also called wong bok, it can be eaten raw in salads, or lightly stir-fried.

Techniques & equipment

With the right techniques and equipment it is easy to cook food with little or no fat. The natural flavours are enhanced and food retains its nutritional value and unmistakable freshness.

Woks

Woks require less oil for cooking, make tossing ingredients easy, and they can hold a bamboo steamer for no-fat steaming. The traditional low-carbon steel variety with two handles is relatively cheap and a good heat conductor. A round base is best for gas stovetops; use flat-bottom for electric or induction stovetops or use a wok-holder ring with holes in it.

Seasoning a wok

Carbon steel woks must be 'seasoned' before first use. Wash in hot, soapy water, rinse and place over medium heat to dry. Wipe with vegetable oil and paper towels; heat on low for 10 minutes; wipe clean. Repeat and wipe off any excess oil. After cooking, rinse the wok without soap, wipe clean, heat to dry completely and lightly oil again to prevent rusting.

Stir-frying in a wok or frying pan

- Preheat the wok over high heat, add oil and heat for 1 minute before adding food.
- Don't overcrowd the wok. Overcrowding drops the temperature, stewing the food, whose juices are released into the wok rather than being sealed into the food.
- Make sure the wok or pan is very hot before adding diced meat or poultry.
- If meat is marinated in yogurt or sweet marinades such as sweet chilli or honey, drain the excess marinade before adding to the wok and cook at a lower temperature so it doesn't burn.
- If oil 'spits' when added to a hot wok, there is probably water in the pan. Partly cover with a lid, allowing the steam to escape until the spitting stops, or add food immediately.

Steamers

Steaming food requires no oil, enhances natural flavours and maintains nutrients. Traditional Asian bamboo steamers with domed lids are cheap and practical, fitting neatly within a wok. Steamers can be stacked and swapped halfway for even cooking, or you can put foods requiring more cooking in the bottom steamer, closer to the heat.

Techniques for steaming

- A wide, shallow steamer allows steam to penetrate the food more efficiently than a deep one. It is better to leave space around and between food for steam to circulate.
- To create sufficient steam, the water underneath must be boiling but not touching the steamer.
- Herbs, spices or vegetables can be added to the steaming liquid; leeks, celery or lemongrass tops placed directly under the food impart flavour.
- Vegetables, such as potatoes, can be cooked in the steaming liquid while other food is being cooked in the steamer above.

Tip To clean a bamboo steamer, wash with a soft brush in warm soapy water, rinse thoroughly and stand in an airy place to dry completely.

Hotpots

Hotpots (Chinese fondues) are a great no-fat cooking method and perfect for entertaining, as all of the preparation is done in advance and the food can be cooked at the table for guests to help themselves.

Cooking in a hotpot

- Prepare any combination of thinly sliced beef, seafood, tofu, vegetables and noodles. Guests add a selection to the simmering stock and serve with dipping sauces, drinking flavoursome stock as soup to finish the meal if desired.
- To cut meat into paper thin slices, partially freeze it first, or ask the butcher to cut it for you. Cutting beef across the grain makes it more tender.

Pestle and mortar

Typically made of granite, hard wood or earthenware, the mortar is the bowl and the pestle is the pounding baton used to crush and grind foods such as grains, herbs and spices. Alternatively, use an electric spice grinder, stick blender or food processor in short bursts to achieve similar results.

Using a pestle and mortar

- Pound the hardest, most fibrous ingredients first. Adding a pinch of salt draws out moisture, making mashing easier.
- Place the mortar over a damp cloth to stop it from slipping on the bench. Wipe with a damp cloth to clean after each use.

Cooking in a parcel

Wrapping food in parcels is perfect for low-fat cooking and helps retain natural moisture, keeping food tender. Wrapping food in banana or cabbage leaves, or using non-stick baking (parchment) paper and then foil, means no oil is required. It is a very healthy way to cook.

- Food parcels can be cooked together but made with different flavours. For example, you can make one with chillies and another without, depending on individual preferences.
- Wrapped food can be baked, pan-fried, steamed or barbecued.
- Use inedible wrappers (such as blanched banana leaves, non-stick baking paper or foil) or edible wrappers (cabbage, lettuce or vine leaves) and present on the plate still wrapped.

Tip Banana leaves, though not eaten, impart a mild flavour. Dip leaves into boiling water to soften before wrapping and secure with kitchen string if needed.

Marinating

Marinades are a great way to impart flavour and are often used to tenderise meat and seafood. Once you pour a marinade over the meat, toss to make sure the marinade coats all surfaces for an even distribution of flavour.

- Follow the suggested marinating times for seafood, otherwise it can start to 'cook' in the marinade if left too long, especially if it contains lemon or lime juice.
- Always be mindful that if marinating for any length of time, food may need to be covered and/or refrigerated and is often best returned to room temperature before cooking.
- When ready to cook, drain marinated food so no excess marinade or liquid goes into the cooking pan.

Wok

Steamer

Pestle and mortar

Appetisers & snacks

Hand-rolled sushi

This type of sushi (temaki zushi) is great fun as all the ingredients are prepared beforehand and guests make their own sushi, without the need for sushi mats. The sushi should be eaten as soon as it's made. Provide each guest with a finger bowl and hand towel.

PREPARATION 30 minutes   COOKING 15 minutes   SERVES 4 (makes 16)

4 sheets nori, cut into quarters

2 teaspoons wasabi (Japanese horseradish)

100 g (3^1/$_2$ oz) sashimi-grade tuna or salmon, thinly sliced

^{1}/$_2$ small Lebanese (short) cucumber, seeded and cut into matchsticks

^{1}/$_2$ small red capsicum (bell pepper), halved, seeded and thinly sliced

^{1}/$_2$ avocado, sliced

2 tablespoons gari (pink pickled ginger)

^{1}/$_3$ cup (80 ml) salt-reduced shoyu (Japanese soy sauce), to serve

SUSHI RICE

1^1/$_4$ cups (275 g) short-grain white rice

2 tablespoons rice vinegar, plus extra for dipping

1 tablespoon caster (superfine) sugar

^{1}/$_2$ teaspoon salt

Each serving (4 pieces) provides
491 kJ, 117 kcal, 7 g protein, 3 g fat
(1 g saturated fat), 14 g carbohydrate
(3 g sugars), <1 g fibre, 600 mg sodium

1 To make the sushi, put the rice into a large bowl, cover with water, stir and drain well. Repeat three more times until the water runs clear. Drain and tip the rice into a saucepan with 1^1/$_2$ cups (375 ml) water, cover with a lid and bring to the boil. Reduce the heat to low and simmer for 12 minutes, or until cooked. Set aside, covered, for 10 minutes.

2 Put the vinegar, sugar and salt in a small saucepan over medium heat and stir until the sugar dissolves. Set aside to cool.

3 Spread the cooked rice in a large non-metallic dish. Use a flat wooden spoon or plastic paddle to break up any lumps, then slowly pour the vinegar evenly over the top. Set aside, turning the rice every 5–10 minutes until cool, then cover with a damp tea towel (dish towel) until needed.

4 Working with one piece of nori at a time, place it in the palm of one hand, shiny-side down. Dip the fingers of your other hand into a bowl of water with a splash of vinegar added, shaking off the excess – this will help to prevent the rice from sticking as you work. Place 1–2 tablespoons of rice in the centre of each nori and spread out to the top corner.

5 To serve, lightly spread a dab of wasabi across the rice and let your guests top each piece with a selection of tuna, cucumber, capsicum, avocado and pickled ginger. Fold each side of the nori across the rice to form a cone – the pointy tip end of the cone can be folded underneath to hold the shape securely, if desired. Dip the nori in shoyu and eat immediately.

ANOTHER IDEA

You can substitute or add other fillings, such as sliced blanched snow peas (mangetout), spinach leaves, green beans, marinated tofu, bamboo shoots, smoked salmon or cooked prawns (shrimp).

Pleated seafood dumplings

With a bit of practice, these Chinese-style dumplings are simple and fun to prepare. Served warm with a dipping sauce, they make a wonderfully tasty snack or appetiser. And because they are steamed, they are light, low fat and healthy.

PREPARATION 25 minutes   COOKING 7 minutes   SERVES 8 (makes 32)

1   In a small bowl, cover the mushrooms in the boiling water and set aside for about 20 minutes, or until softened. Drain well, discard the stems and finely chop the caps.

2   Mix the mushrooms, prawns, spring onions, garlic, ginger, salt, water chestnuts, soy sauce, sherry, sesame oil and cornflour in a mixing bowl.

3   Take 1 teaspoon of the mixture at a time and place in the centre of a won ton wrapper. Fold the wrapper over to enclose the filling and gently pleat the edges together to seal and enclose the filling. Repeat with the remaining filling and wrappers to make 32 dumplings in total.

4   Working in batches, arrange the dumplings in a single layer in a bamboo steamer. Cover and steam over a wok of simmering water for 5–7 minutes, or until the filling is firm and cooked through.

5   To make the dipping sauce, whisk together the soy sauce, molasses, sugar and lime juice in a small bowl and serve with the dumplings.

ANOTHER IDEA
You can substitute half of the prawn meat with minced (ground) pork if you wish. You can also serve the dumplings with the Asian dipping sauce on page 246.

6 dried Chinese or European mushrooms

$^1/_2$ cup (125 ml) boiling water

250 g (8 oz) minced raw prawns (ground uncooked shrimp meat)

2 spring onions (scallions), thinly sliced

1 clove garlic, crushed

1 tablespoon grated fresh ginger

$^1/_4$ teaspoon salt

$^1/_4$ cup (45 g) finely chopped canned water chestnuts

1 tablespoon soy sauce

1 tablespoon dry sherry

1 teaspoon sesame oil (optional)

2 teaspoons cornflour (cornstarch)

32 won ton wrappers

DIPPING SAUCE

2 tablespoons salt-reduced soy sauce

1 tablespoon molasses

2 teaspoons dark brown sugar

1 tablespoon fresh lime juice

Each serving (4 dumplings) provides
834 kJ, 200 kcal, 12 g protein, <1 g fat
(<1 g saturated fat), 35 g carbohydrate
(5 g sugars), 2 g fibre, 728 mg sodium

Steamed vegetables with peanut dip

This healthy snack combines the natural flavours of lightly steamed crisp vegetables with a deliciously tasty peanut sauce. It is a great way of using leftover vegetables and can be adapted to include any fresh produce that is in season.

PREPARATION 20 minutes   COOKING 10 minutes   SERVES 8

16 baby carrots with tops, peeled

2 large red or yellow capsicums (bell peppers), halved, seeded and sliced

250 g (8 oz) snow peas (mangetout) or green beans, trimmed

8 radishes, thinly sliced

PEANUT DIP

1/3 cup (100 g) salt-reduced smooth peanut butter

1 clove garlic, crushed

2 teaspoons grated fresh ginger

2 spring onions (scallions), chopped

2 tablespoons soft brown sugar

2 tablespoons soy sauce

1 pinch chilli powder

1 tablespoon fresh lemon juice

Each serving provides
504 kJ, 120 kcal, 6 g protein, 7 g fat
(1 g saturated fat), 10 g carbohydrate
(8 g sugars), 4 g fibre, 428 mg sodium

1 To make the peanut dip, put $2/3$ cup (150 ml) water in a small saucepan and bring to the boil. Reduce the heat to medium-low and stir in the peanut butter, garlic, ginger, spring onions, sugar, soy sauce and chilli powder. Simmer for 2 minutes, then remove from heat and stir in the lemon juice. Refrigerate until ready to serve.

2 Fill a large saucepan with water and bring to the boil. Put the carrots into a steamer basket and cook for 3 minutes, then lift out and plunge immediately into a bowl of iced water to refresh.

3 Steam the capsicums for 1 minute, then refresh immediately in a bowl of iced water. Steam the snow peas for 2 minutes, then refresh immediately in a bowl of iced water. Drain all of the vegetables and dry with paper towels.

4 Arrange the carrot sticks, capsicums and snow peas in a serving bowl and garnish with the sliced radish. Serve with the peanut dip passed separately.

ANOTHER IDEA

You can use just about any vegetables to serve with this peanut dip. Try raw celery or cucumber, sliced into matchsticks, or lightly steamed florets of cauliflower or broccoli if you prefer.

Lamb and plum wraps

Packed with crisp raw vegetables and juicy fruit slices, these wraps make a refreshing alternative to duck in this popular Chinese snack. They are ideal for entertaining because the lamb is equally good served hot or at room temperature, while the wraps themselves make for tasty, fuss-free eating.

PREPARATION 35 minutes   COOKING 10 minutes   SERVES 4 (makes 16 wraps)

1 To make the sesame dipping sauce, put all of the ingredients into a screw-top jar and shake well. Set aside until needed.

2 Put the lamb slices in a bowl with the soy sauce and set aside to marinate.

3 Rinse and dry the lettuce leaves and remove the central stalks. Tear off 16 pieces large enough to fit in the centre of the rice paper wrappers. Finely shred the remaining lettuce and set aside.

4 Heat a wok or large non-stick frying pan over a medium-high heat. Add half of the lamb slices and stir-fry for 3-5 minutes, or until the meat is cooked to your liking. Remove to a plate and keep warm while cooking the remaining lamb.

5 Working with one wrapper at a time, dip the rice wrapper into a bowl of hot water to soften for 20-25 seconds, then transfer to clean tea towel (dish towel) and pat dry. Place a trimmed lettuce leaf in the centre of the wrapper and top with a few lamb slices, some spring onions cucumber, plum slices and shredded lettuce. Fold in both sides of the wrapper, then roll up neatly tucking in one end, and set aside. Repeat with the remaining wrappers and filling ingredients to make 16 wraps in total.

6 Arrange the wraps on a serving platter and scatter over any remaining spring onion. Serve with the dipping sauce passed separately.

HEALTHY EATING

Although lamb still tends to contain more fat than other meats, changes in breeding, feeding and butchery techniques mean that lean cuts only contain about one-third of the fat that they would have 20 years ago. More of the fat is monounsaturated, which is good news for healthy hearts.

500 g (1 lb) lean lamb neck fillets or other lean lamb meat, trimmed of fat, thinly sliced

1 1/2 tablespoons salt-reduced soy sauce

16 large cos (romaine) lettuce leaves, trimmed

16 rice paper wrappers

6 spring onions (scallions), thinly sliced lengthwise

1/4 telegraph (long) cucumber, halved lengthwise, seeded and thinly sliced

6 sweet red plums, halved, stones removed and thinly sliced

SESAME DIPPING SAUCE

1 tablespoon sesame oil

1 tablespoon grated fresh ginger

2 teaspoons sesame seeds

2 teaspoons salt-reduced soy sauce

1 teaspoon caster (superfine) sugar

Each serving (4 wraps) provides
1890 kJ, 450 kcal, 30 g protein, 13 g fat (4 g saturated fat), 15 g carbohydrate (11 g sugars), 4 g fibre, 506 mg sodium

Thai fish cakes

These tasty fish cakes are a popular Thai dish that can be made in advance and stored in the refrigerator. They are perfect for entertaining, as they can be cooked indoors or on a barbecue and are easy to pass around at parties.

PREPARATION 15 minutes   COOKING 10 minutes   SERVES 4 (makes 12)

500 g (1 lb) boneless, skinless, firm white fish fillets, cut into chunks

2 tablespoons red curry paste (see page 248)

1^1/$_2$ tablespoons fish sauce

10 green beans, trimmed and thinly sliced

^{1}/$_3$ cup (15 g) chopped fresh coriander (cilantro) leaves

1-2 tablespoons vegetable or peanut oil

DIPPING SAUCE

^{1}/$_4$ cup (55 g) sugar

^{1}/$_4$ cup (60 ml) coconut vinegar or white vinegar

1 long red chilli, seeded and finely chopped

1 tablespoon fish sauce

2 tablespoons fresh coriander (cilantro) leaves, chopped

Each serving (3 cakes) provides
386 kJ, 92 kcal, 9 g protein, 4 g fat
(1 g saturated fat), 6 g carbohydrate
(5 g sugars), <1 g fibre, 420 mg sodium

1   Put the fish into a food processor and pulse for 30 seconds. Add the curry paste and fish sauce and pulse until the mixture is just combined. Transfer to a bowl and add the beans and coriander and stir to combine. Divide the mixture into 12 portions and shape each portion into a thin patty. Cover with plastic wrap and refrigerate until needed.

2   To make the dipping sauce, put the sugar, vinegar and ^{1}/$_4$ cup (60 ml) water in a small saucepan over medium heat. Stir for 2-3 minutes, or until the sugar has dissolved. Remove from heat, cool, then stir in the chilli, fish sauce and coriander. Set aside.

3   Heat the vegetable oil in a large frying pan over a medium heat. Cook the fish cakes, in batches, for 3-4 minutes on each side, or until cooked through. Serve immediately with the dipping sauce on the side.

ANOTHER IDEA

Redfish is traditionally used to make fish cakes because the chopped flesh holds together well. If using other fish, such as flathead, blue eye or ling, you can add 1 lightly beaten egg white to hold the cakes together.

Beef skewers with ginger dipping sauce

PREPARATION 25 minutes, plus 30 minutes soaking   COOKING 15 minutes   SERVES 6 (makes 24)

350 g (12 oz) sirloin steak, cut 3 cm
   (1¼ inch) thick, trimmed of fat
3 yellow capsicums (bell peppers), cut
   into small triangles
4 spring onions (scallions), cut into
   8 cm (3¼ inch) lengths

GINGER DIPPING SAUCE
½ cup (125 ml) rice vinegar
½ cup (60 g) finely chopped red
   capsicum (bell pepper)
2 tablespoons caster (superfine) sugar
1 tablespoon chopped Asian shallots or
   red onion
1½ teaspoons grated fresh ginger
1½ teaspoons chilli sauce
½ teaspoon finely grated lemon zest

Each serving (4 skewers) provides
590 kJ, 141 kcal, 13 g protein, 4 g fat
(2 g saturated fat), 9 g carbohydrate
(9 g sugars), <1 g fibre, 51 mg sodium

1   Soak 24 wooden skewers in water for 30 minutes to prevent
    them from burning during cooking. Freeze the steak for
    20 minutes.

2   To make the ginger dipping sauce, mix together all of the
    ingredients in a small serving bowl and set aside.

3   Blanch the capsicums in a saucepan of boiling water for
    1 minute. Drain, then rinse with cold water and pat dry with
    paper towels. Toss in a bowl with 2 tablespoons of the
    dipping sauce.

4   Preheat a barbecue chargrill plate or a grill (broiler) to high.
    Slice the steak into 24 very thin strips, then thread a steak
    strip, a capsicum triangle and a piece of spring onion onto
    each skewer, twisting the meat round the vegetables. Grill
    for 3-5 minutes on each side, or until cooked through. Serve
    immediately, with the dipping sauce passed separately.

ANOTHER IDEA

Instead of the ginger dipping sauce you can serve these skewers
with the spicy chilli jam recipe on page 249. You can replace the
steak with cubes of firm tofu for a vegetarian option.

Seafood sesame toasts

PREPARATION 15 minutes   COOKING 25 minutes   SERVES 4

1 Preheat the oven to 200ºC (400ºF/Gas 6) and lightly grease a baking tray.

2 To make the topping, place the prawn meat, crabmeat, spring onions, garlic, capsicum, lemon zest, cayenne pepper and 1 tablespoon of the cream into a bowl and mix together to make a spreadable paste. Season with pepper and set aside until needed. (The prawn mixture can be prepared in advance and stored in the refrigerator for up to 4 hours.)

3 Put the remaining cream and the egg in a bowl and beat until smooth. Working with one slice of bread at a time, dip it into the egg mixture to coat, then place on the prepared tray. Spread the prawn and crab topping evenly over the bread. Lightly brush the remaining egg and cream mixture over the top and evenly sprinkle over the sesame seeds.

4 Bake the toasts for 20-25 minutes, or until they are crisp and golden. Cut each slice of toast into 8 small triangles and serve immediately, while still hot, garnished with spring onion.

85 g (3 oz) minced raw prawns
  (uncooked ground shrimp meat)
85 g (3 oz) fresh crabmeat, flaked
2 spring onions (scallions), thinly sliced
1 clove garlic, crushed
1/2 small red capsicum (bell pepper),
  seeded and diced
1/2 teaspoon finely grated lemon zest
1/8 teaspoon cayenne pepper
2 tablespoons low-fat thickened
  (whipping) cream
1 egg
2 slices wholemeal (wholewheat) bread
2 teaspoons sesame seeds
spring onion (scallion), thinly sliced
  lengthwise, to garnish

Each serving provides
668 kJ, 160 kcal, 12 g protein, 6 g fat
(3 g saturated fat), 12 g carbohydrate
(2 g sugars), 2 g fibre, 185 mg sodium

HEALTHY EATING

Crabmeat is low in saturated fat and has many nutrition benefits for heart-conscious people. It contains high levels of omega-3 fatty acids and is rich in B vitamins and many minerals.

Pork dumplings with peanut salad

These fragrant Chinese-style pot-stickers are made with won ton wrappers. They are part fried, then simmered in stock and served on a bed of green leaves with a spicy salad of peanuts and crunchy vegetables, making the perfect snack or starter.

PREPARATION 30 minutes   COOKING 15 minutes   SERVES 4 (makes 20)

1   Put the pork into a bowl with the water chestnuts, spring onions, ginger, hoisin sauce and soy sauce and use your hands to mix together until well combined. Divide the mixture into 20 equal portions.

2   Working with one won ton wrapper at a time, brush with the beaten egg and place a portion of the pork mixture in the centre. Gather up the wrapper around the pork and squeeze it together at the top to seal in the filling and form an old-fashioned moneybag shape. Repeat with the remaining pork and won ton wrappers.

3   Heat the canola oil in a large frying pan over medium heat. Arrange the dumplings in the base of the pan in a single layer. Cover and cook for 5 minutes, or until they are lightly browned on the base.

4   Pour in enough of the hot stock to come halfway up the sides of the dumplings, then re-cover the pan and simmer gently for 10 minutes, or until the won ton wrappers are cooked through. Drain well on paper towels.

5   Meanwhile, to make the spicy peanut salad, toss the cucumber, carrot, shallots and coriander together in a bowl. Gradually add the sweet chilli sauce, to taste, then add the peanuts and season with black pepper.

6   To serve, arrange the lettuce leaves on serving plates and spoon in some of the spicy peanut salad. Top with the dumplings and garnish with coriander.

ANOTHER IDEA

You can substitute minced raw prawns (ground uncooked shrimp meat) for the pork in these dumplings or a combination of the two for a tempting variation.

250 g (8 oz) lean minced (ground) pork
1/4 cup (45 g) finely chopped canned water chestnuts
3 spring onions (scallions), finely chopped
1 tablespoon grated fresh ginger
2 tablespoons hoisin sauce
1 tablespoon salt-reduced soy sauce
20 won ton wrappers
1 egg, beaten
2 tablespoons canola oil
1¼ cups (310 ml) salt-reduced chicken stock, heated

SPICY PEANUT SALAD

7 cm (3 inch) piece cucumber, halved, seeded and finely diced
1 large carrot, finely diced
2 Asian shallots or 1/2 small red onion, finely chopped
2–3 tablespoons chopped fresh coriander (cilantro) leaves
2 tablespoons sweet chilli sauce (see page 246)
4 tablespoons finely chopped unsalted peanuts
4–8 crisp green lettuce leaves, to serve
sprigs of fresh coriander (cilantro), to garnish

Each serving (5 dumplings) provides
2067 kJ, 494 kcal, 25 g protein, 21 g fat (3 g saturated fat), 50 g carbohydrate (10 g sugars), 5 g fibre, 1105 mg sodium

Crispy prawn tartlets

PREPARATION 35 minutes   COOKING 12–15 minutes   SERVES 4 (makes 12)

1 tablespoon sunflower oil

1 teaspoon sesame oil

3 sheets filo pastry, 30 x 50 cm
(12 x 20 inches) each

1 clove garlic, crushed

3 spring onions (scallions), thinly sliced

1 tablespoon grated fresh ginger

1 carrot, cut into fine julienne

300 g (10 oz) raw tiger prawns
(uncooked large shrimp), peeled and
deveined

75 g (2¹/₂ oz) snowpeas (mangetout),
thinly sliced

1 bok choy, leaves separated

75 g (2¹/₂ oz) bean sprouts

1 tablespoon light soy sauce

sprigs of fresh coriander (cilantro),
to garnish

Each serving (3 tartlets) provides
765 kJ, 183 kcal, 18 g protein, 7 g fat
(<1 g saturated fat), 10 g carbohydrate
(2 g sugars), 2 g fibre, 381 mg sodium

1   Preheat the oven to 200°C (400°F/Gas 6). Lightly grease a 12-hole standard muffin tin. Mix together the sunflower and sesame oils. Trim the pastry sheets to make a 30 x 40 cm (12 x 16 inch) rectangle, discarding the excess pastry. Cut it lengthwise into three pieces, then widthwise into quarters to create thirty-six 10 cm (4 inch) squares.

2   Place a square of filo pastry into the base of each muffin hole. Brush the oil mixture lightly over the top, then place another square of filo over the first, arranging it so the corners are not directly on top of those beneath. Brush with a little more oil, then place a third layer of filo on top with the corners offset. Bake the pastry cases for 5–7 minutes, or until golden brown and crisp.

3   Meanwhile, heat the remaining oil mixture in a wok or large frying pan over medium heat. Add the garlic, spring onions and ginger, and stir-fry for about 30 seconds. Add the carrot and stir-fry for 2 minutes, then add the prawns and stir-fry for a further 2 minutes, or until they turn pink.

4   Add the snowpeas, bok choy and bean sprouts and stir-fry for 2–3 minutes, or until all the vegetables are just tender. Add the soy sauce and toss to combine.

5   Spoon the prawn and vegetable mixture into the filo pastry cases and serve immediately, garnished with the coriander.

Thai-style crab cakes

PREPARATION 20 minutes   COOKING 15 minutes   SERVES 4 (makes 12)

1   Place the crabmeat and fish in a food processor or blender and process until well combined. Add the curry paste, kaffir lime leaf, coriander, sugar, salt and egg. Process again to combine. Divide the mixture into 12 even-sized pieces and roll each into a ball. Flatten slightly to make a patty, then cover and refrigerate until needed.

2   To make the sweet and sour dipping sauce, put the vinegar, sugar, fish sauce and 2 tablespoons water in a small saucepan over medium heat and stir until the sugar dissolves. Bring to the boil and boil for 2–3 minutes, or until syrupy, then remove from the heat and cool. Stir through the chilli.

3   Mix together the carrots, cucumber and spring onions in a serving bowl.

4   Heat the oil in a large non-stick frying pan. Fry the crab cakes for 2–3 minutes on each side, or until golden and cooked through. Drain on paper towels. Serve the crab cakes with the carrot and cucumber salad, lime wedges and dipping sauce on the side. Garnish with coriander.

350 g (12 oz) crabmeat

250 g (8 oz) skinless white fish fillets, such as cod or haddock, cut into chunks

1 tablespoon red curry paste (see page 248)

1 fresh kaffir lime (makrut) leaf or grated zest of $1/2$ lime

2 tablespoons chopped fresh coriander (cilantro) leaves

$1/2$ teaspoon caster (superfine) sugar

1 pinch salt

1 egg, beaten

2 carrots, finely chopped

$1/2$ cucumber, finely chopped

4 spring onions (scallions), finely chopped

2 tablespoons sunflower oil

lime wedges, to garnish

sprigs of fresh coriander (cilantro), to garnish

SWEET AND SOUR DIPPING SAUCE

3 tablespoons white wine or cider vinegar

50 g ($1^3/4$ oz) caster (superfine) sugar

1 tablespoon fish sauce

1 long red chilli, seeded and finely chopped

Each serving (3 crab cakes) provides
1315 kJ, 314 kcal, 30 g protein, 13 g fat (2 g saturated fat), 17 g carbohydrate (16 g sugars), 2 g fibre, 950 mg sodium

Chicken yakitori skewers

These traditional Japanese chicken skewers are first marinated in a sweetened soy sauce mixture with fresh ginger, giving them a vibrant and unique flavour that is hard to resist. They are perfect for entertaining and make a delicious snack or starter.

PREPARATION 25 minutes, plus 1 hour marinating   COOKING 15-20 minutes   SERVES 15 (makes 30)

3 tablespoons shoyu (Japanese soy sauce)
3 tablespoons sake or dry sherry
1 tablespoon sesame oil
1 clove garlic, crushed
1 tablespoon grated fresh ginger
2 teaspoons honey
500 g (1 lb) skinless, boneless chicken breast fillets, cut into 2 cm ($^3/_4$ inch) cubes
1 large green capsicum (bell pepper), seeded and cut into 2 cm ($^3/_4$ inch) cubes
4 spring onions (scallions), cut into 2 cm ($^3/_4$ inch) lengths
vegetable oil, for cooking

Each serving (2 skewers) provides
1036 kJ, 248 kcal, 28 g protein, 12 g fat (2 g saturated fat), 6 g carbohydrate (6 g sugars), 1 g fibre, 286 mg sodium

1   Place the shoyu, sake, sesame oil, garlic, ginger and honey into a shallow, non-metallic dish and stir well to combine. Add the chicken, turning to coat in the marinade. Cover and refrigerate for at least 1 hour, or overnight.

2   Soak 30 small wooden or bamboo skewers in cold water for 30 minutes to prevent them from burning during cooking. Preheat a chargrill pan or barbecue hotplate over medium-high heat.

3   Thread 2 pieces of the chicken onto each skewer, alternating with the capsicum and spring onions. Lightly oil the pan with vegetable oil and cook the chicken skewers, in batches, for about 10-15 minutes, turning from time to time and brushing with the marinade, until cooked through. Serve immediately.

HEALTHY EATING

A great source of protein and B-group vitamins, chicken contains less saturated fat than the equivalent amount of beef, making it a healthy alternative. The breast is the leanest part of the chicken.

Noodles & rice

Low-fat laksa

This spicy noodle soup is popular in Malaysia, Singapore and the Philippines. It is a hearty soup that makes a substantial main meal and can easily be varied to suit your preference. Try chicken or fried tofu instead of the salmon.

PREPARATION 10 minutes   COOKING 20 minutes   SERVES 4

250 g (8 oz) dried cellophane noodles (Chinese vermicelli)

1/4 cup (70 g) laksa paste

4 cups (1 litre) salt-reduced chicken stock

1 cup (250 ml) low-fat coconut milk

1 stem lemongrass, white part only, bruised

500 g (8 oz) skinless salmon fillets, cut into small chunks

500 g (8 oz) bok choy, coarsely chopped

1 tablespoon fresh lime juice

3 cups (270 g) bean sprouts, trimmed

1/2 cup (15 g) fresh coriander (cilantro) leaves

lime wedges, to serve

Each serving provides
2360 kJ, 564 kcal, 39 g protein, 20 g fat (10 g saturated fat), 56 g carbohydrate (7 g sugars), 3 g fibre, 717 mg sodium

1   Cook the noodles in a saucepan of boiling water for 3 minutes, or until tender. Drain well and set aside.

2   Put the laksa paste, stock, coconut milk and lemongrass into a large saucepan and bring to the boil, stirring to combine. Reduce the heat to medium-low and simmer for 10 minutes. Add the salmon and simmer for 2–3 minutes, or until the salmon flakes easily when tested with a fork. Add the bok choy and lime juice and cook for a further 2 minutes, or until the bok choy has wilted.

3   Divide the noodles and bean sprouts among serving bowls and pour over the soup. Sprinkle over the coriander and serve immediately with the lime wedges on the side for squeezing over.

ANOTHER IDEA
You can substitute the salmon with prawns (shrimp) or thinly sliced chicken breast fillet and add an extra 2–3 minutes to the cooking time. You can also use rice vermicelli instead of the cellophane noodles if you prefer.

Noodles & rice

40

Chinese seafood noodles

PREPARATION 15 minutes   COOKING 10-12 minutes   SERVES 4

200 g (7 oz) wok-ready hokkien (egg)
    noodles
2 teaspoons sesame oil
3 tablespoons vegetable oil
5 spring onions (scallions), chopped
2 cloves garlic, crushed
1 long green chilli, seeded and chopped
4 cups (250 g) mixed frozen stir-fry
    vegetables
1$^{1}/_{4}$ cups (310 ml) salt-reduced
    vegetable stock
1$^{2}/_{3}$ cups (150 g) sliced button mushrooms
1$^{2}/_{3}$ cups (150 g) bean sprouts, trimmed
300 g (10 oz) raw prawns (uncooked
    shrimp), peeled and deveined
2 tablespoons salt-reduced soy sauce
3 eggs, beaten

Each serving provides
2148 kJ, 513 kcal, 32 g protein, 22 g fat
(4 g saturated fat), 43 g carbohydrate
(1 g sugars), 1 g fibre, 175 mg sodium

1   Soak the noodles according to the packet instructions. Drain
    well, then toss with the sesame oil to coat and set aside.

2   Heat 1 tablespoon of the vegetable oil in a wok or large
    non-stick frying pan. Add the spring onions, garlic, chilli and
    mixed vegetables and stir-fry for 3 minutes. Add the stock
    and bring to the boil, then add the mushrooms and sprouts
    and cook for 2-3 minutes, or until the vegetables are just
    cooked and most of the stock is absorbed.

3   Add the prawns to the pan, stir in the soy sauce and cook
    for 3 minutes, or until the prawns start to turn pink. Add
    the noodles and toss to combine until heated through.

4   Meanwhile, heat the remaining vegetable oil in a small frying
    pan. Season the eggs with salt and black pepper and stir
    gently until the eggs have set into large, soft curds. Mix
    into the noodles and serve immediately.

HEALTHY EATING

You can use any combination of stir-fry vegetables in this dish,
but the addition of broccoli is recommended as it is one of the
best sources of vitamin C and offers beneficial antioxidants.

Egg fried rice

PREPARATION 10 minutes   COOKING 30 minutes   SERVES 4

1 Put the rice into a large saucepan with 3 cups (750 ml) water and 1 teaspoon of the vegetable oil. Bring to the boil, then reduce the heat, cover, and simmer for 10–15 minutes, or until the liquid has been absorbed and the rice is cooked.

2 Meanwhile, heat 1 tablespoon of the vegetable oil in a wok or large non-stick frying pan over medium heat. Add the eggs and swirl the wok to make a thin omelette. Cook the eggs until set. Remove to a plate, cool and thinly slice.

3 Add the remaining oil to the wok and cook the bacon over medium heat until cooked through. Add the carrots, reduce the heat and cook for 2 minutes. Add the spring onions, garlic and peas and cook for a further 2 minutes.

4 Add the prawns to the wok, turn up the heat, and cook for 3–4 minutes, or until they start to turn pink and are cooked through, then add the bean sprouts and toss well to combine.

5 Add the rice and egg to the wok, then pour in the soy sauce, sake, mirin and sesame oil and mix well to combine and coat the rice. Stir-fry over high heat for a further 5 minutes, or until the mixture is dry. Serve immediately.

2 cups (400 g) long-grain white rice
2 tablespoons vegetable oil
4 eggs, beaten
250 g (8 oz) slices rindless bacon (bacon strips), trimmed and chopped
3 carrots, diced
8 spring onions (scallions), thinly sliced
2 cloves garlic, crushed
1½ cups (200 g) frozen baby peas
250 g (8 oz) raw prawns (uncooked shrimp), peeled and deveined
2 cups (180 g) bean sprouts, trimmed
3 tablespoons salt-reduced soy sauce
3 tablespoons sake or dry sherry
3 tablespoons mirin or 1 teaspoon honey
1 tablespoon sesame oil

Each serving provides
3763 kJ, 900 kcal, 44 g protein, 26 g fat (6 g saturated fat), 87 g carbohydrate (7 g sugars), 4 g fibre, 1645 mg sodium

ANOTHER IDEA

If you prefer, you can omit the prawns in this dish and replace them with cubes of firm tofu. You will need to cook the tofu in a separate pan in a little vegetable oil for about 5 minutes, stirring regularly, until lightly golden on all sides. Return to the pan with the egg to heat through before serving.

Noodles & rice

43

Vietnamese broth with noodles

Punchy flavours and aromatic ingredients transform a light broth into an exotic dish that makes a substantial light meal. The ingredients are not fried before being simmered, making this a great low-fat soup. For best results, select prime-quality lean steak, which tastes excellent when poached.

PREPARATION 10 minutes, plus 20 minutes soaking   COOKING 10–15 minutes   SERVES 2

1 cup (20 g) dried shiitake mushrooms

75 g (2¹/₂ oz) rice vermicelli

175 g (6 oz) lean rump (round) steak, diced

2 cups (500 ml) salt-reduced beef stock

2 tablespoons fish sauce

1 teaspoon grated fresh ginger

¹/₃ cup (30 g) bean sprouts, trimmed

¹/₂ small onion, thinly sliced

2 spring onions (scallions), thinly sliced

2 small red birdseye (Thai) chillies, seeded and finely chopped

1 tablespoon finely chopped fresh mint

1 tablespoon finely chopped fresh coriander (cilantro) leaves

1 tablespoon finely chopped fresh basil

lime wedges, to serve

soy sauce (optional), to serve

Each serving provides
1447 kJ, 345 kcal, 29 g protein, 5 g fat (2 g saturated fat), 46 g carbohydrate (7 g sugars), 4 g fibre, 2947 mg sodium

1   Soak the shiitake mushrooms in a bowl of boiling water for 20 minutes. Drain and reserve the soaking liquid. Discard the stem and finely slice the caps. Meanwhile, soak the noodles according to the packet instructions. Drain well and set aside until needed.

2   Put the reserved mushroom soaking liquid into a large saucepan over high heat. Add the mushrooms, steak, stock, fish sauce and ginger and bring to the boil. Reduce the heat and simmer for 10–15 minutes, or until the steak is tender, skimming off any impurities that rise to the surface.

3   Divide the noodles, bean sprouts and onion between two large serving bowls. Use a slotted spoon to remove the steak and mushrooms from the broth and divide them between the bowls. Ladle the broth into the bowls, then scatter the spring onions, chilli, mint, coriander and basil over the top. Serve immediately with the lime wedges – the juice can be squeezed into the broth, to taste. Soy sauce can also be added, if desired.

ANOTHER IDEA

The bean sprouts can be replaced by shavings of carrot and chopped celery. Vary the quantities of spring onion, chilli and fresh herbs to taste. For a warm, spicy flavour, add a good pinch of ground cinnamon with the ginger.

Teriyaki-style noodles with tofu

This rich, Japanese-style broth, flavoured with vibrant fresh herbs, ginger and garlic, peps up firm tofu and long strands of earthy buckwheat noodles. You could also add fresh bok choy to the mix of vegetables.

PREPARATION 15 minutes   COOKING 10 minutes   SERVES 2

1 Cook the soba noodles in a saucepan of boiling water for about 6 minutes, or until al dente. Drain well and set aside.

2 Blanch the mixed vegetables in a separate saucepan of boiling water until tender. Drain and set aside.

3 Put the stock, soy sauce, mirin, tofu, spring onions, chilli, fresh herbs, garlic and ginger in a large saucepan with 150 ml (5 fl oz) water and bring to the boil. Reduce the heat to low, add the noodles and vegetables to the pan and simmer very briefly until they are heated through.

4 Divide the vegetables, tofu and broth between deep serving bowls and serve immediately.

HEALTHY EATING

Tofu is an excellent source of soy protein, making it a great choice for vegetarians or people who would like to reduce the amount of meat in their diet. It is also a good source of iron, copper and manganese and is often enriched with calcium.

125 g (4 oz) soba (Japanese buckwheat noodles)

2 cups (125 g) mixed frozen stir-fry vegetables

150 ml (5 fl oz) salt-reduced vegetable stock

1 tablespoon salt-reduced soy sauce

$1/3$ cup (80 ml) mirin or dry sherry

$1^2/3$ cups (300 g) cubed firm tofu

2 spring onions (scallions), chopped

1 long red chilli, seeded and chopped

1 tablespoon chopped fresh mint

1 tablespoon chopped fresh coriander (cilantro) leaves

1 clove garlic, crushed

$1/2$ teaspoon grated fresh ginger

Each serving provides
2070 kJ, 494 kcal, 31 g protein, 12 g fat (2 g saturated fat), 54 g carbohydrate (9 g sugars), 6 g fibre, 1475 mg sodium

Noodles & rice

47

Stir-fried beef with noodles

Tangy tamarind and lemongrass infuse a Thai-inspired sauce for tender strips of beef and fine rice noodles. With fresh greens and baby corn adding the all-important vegetable balance, this is a quick and easy dish that is a meal in itself.

PREPARATION 15 minutes   COOKING 10 minutes   SERVES 2

1 teaspoon tamarind paste

1/4 cup (60 ml) boiling water

2 tablespoons salt-reduced soy sauce

2 teaspoons sesame oil

1 tablespoon mirin or dry sherry

100 g (3 1/2 oz) rice vermicelli

1 tablespoon sunflower oil

225 g (8 oz) lean rump (round) steak, sliced

1 small onion, cut into wedges

2 teaspoons chopped lemongrass

1 long red chilli, seeded and chopped

2 cloves garlic, crushed

3/4 cup (80 g) snow peas (mangetout), halved diagonally

6 fresh or canned baby corn, sliced

1 cup (100 g) sliced fresh shiitake or button mushrooms

Each serving provides
2180 kJ, 521 kcal, 36 g protein, 20 g fat
(4 g saturated fat), 51 g carbohydrate
(6 g sugars), 4 g fibre, 980 mg sodium

1 In a small bowl, combine the tamarind paste and boiling water and leave to soak for 10 minutes, stirring frequently to break down the paste. Mix the resulting tamarind liquid with the soy sauce, sesame oil and mirin.

2 Meanwhile, soak the noodles according to the packet instructions. Drain well and set aside until needed.

3 Heat the sunflower oil in a wok or very large frying pan over high heat. Add the steak and stir-fry for 3 minutes, or until cooked through. Remove to a plate.

4 Add the onion, lemongrass, chilli and garlic to the wok and stir-fry over high heat for 1–2 minutes. Add the snow peas, baby corn and mushrooms, and continue stir-frying for a further 2 minutes, or until cooked.

5 Return the steak to the wok. Add the tamarind liquid and the noodles and stir for about 1 minute, tossing well to combine and heat through. Divide the noodles, steak and vegetables between serving bowls and serve immediately.

ANOTHER IDEA

You can create a vegetarian alternative to this dish by omitting the beef and adding the same amount of firm tofu, cut into 2 cm (3/4 inch) cubes; cook for about 4 minutes, turning often.

Noodles & rice

Yakitori domburi

PREPARATION 15 minutes, plus at least 4 hours marinating   COOKING 25 minutes   SERVES 4

4 x 150 g (5 oz) skinless, boneless chicken breast fillets
2 tablespoons salt-reduced soy sauce
$1/3$ cup (80 ml) mirin
2 teaspoons grated fresh ginger
1 clove garlic, chopped
2 cups (440 g) short-grain white rice
1 tablespoon vegetable oil
2 tablespoons sugar
300 g (10 oz) baby bok choy
2 spring onions (scallions), thinly sliced

Each serving provides
2998 kJ, 716 kcal, 38 g protein, 21 g fat
(5 g saturated fat), 90 g carbohydrate
(11 g sugars), 2 g fibre, 470 mg sodium

1   In a glass bowl, combine the chicken breast fillets, soy sauce, mirin, 2 tablespoons water, ginger and garlic. Cover and refrigerate for at least 4 hours.

2   Wash the rice several times in fresh water until the water runs clear. Drain, then add to a saucepan with 3 cups (750 ml) fresh water. Cover and bring to the boil, then reduce the heat to low and simmer for 12-14 minutes, or until all the water has been absorbed. Remove from the heat and allow the rice to stand, covered, for 10 minutes.

3   Meanwhile, remove the chicken from the marinade, reserving the marinade. Heat the vegetable oil in a wok or large non-stick frying pan over medium heat. Add the chicken and cook for about 5 minutes on each side, or until cooked through. Remove from the heat and slice the chicken into 1 cm ($1/2$ inch) thick slices. Set aside and keep warm.

4   Add the reserved marinade to the same wok with the sugar and 1 cup (250 ml) water. Bring to the boil, then reduce the heat and simmer for 1-2 minutes, skimming off any impurities that rise to the surface. Add the bok choy and spring onions and cook for 1 minute.

5   Divide the rice among serving bowls, top with the chicken, bok choy and a little broth and serve immediately.

Chilli and rice stick noodle stir-fry

PREPARATION 15 minutes   COOKING 10 minutes   SERVES 4

1   Soak the noodles according to the packet instructions. Drain well and set aside.

2   Heat 1 tablespoon of the sunflower oil in a wok or large non-stick frying pan over medium-high heat. Add the prawns and stir-fry for 3-4 minutes, or until they start to turn pink. Remove to a plate.

3   Heat the remaining sunflower oil in the wok over medium heat. Add the garlic, chilli and ginger and stir-fry for a few seconds to flavour the oil. Add the asparagus, sugar snap peas and water chestnuts and stir-fry for about 3 minutes, or until the vegetables start to soften. Add the spring onions and ground coriander and stir well to combine.

4   In a bowl, mix together the fish sauce, honey, cornflour and 2 tablespoons water. Add to the wok and stir gently until the liquid boils and thickens.

5   Return the prawns to the wok, then add the noodles and coriander leaves. Toss gently until the ingredients are well combined and the prawns and noodles are heated through. Divide among serving bowls and serve immediately.

200 g (7 oz) dried rice stick noodles

2 tablespoons sunflower oil

200 g (7 oz) raw tiger prawns (uncooked large shrimp), peeled and deveined, tails left intact

3 cloves garlic, crushed

1 long red chilli, seeded and sliced

1 tablespoon grated fresh ginger

6 asparagus spears, trimmed and cut into 5 cm (2 inch) lengths

1 cup (150 g) chopped sugar snap peas

$3/4$ cup (140 g) water chestnuts, halved

4 spring onions (scallions), sliced

2 teaspoons ground coriander

2 tablespoons fish sauce

1 tablespoon honey

1 teaspoon cornflour (cornstarch)

1 tablespoon finely chopped fresh coriander (cilantro) leaves

Each serving provides
1656 kJ, 396 kcal, 15 g protein, 11 g fat (1 g saturated fat), 57 g carbohydrate (10 g sugars), 4 g fibre, 1092 mg sodium

ANOTHER IDEA

Use 2 skinless, boneless chicken breast fillets instead of the prawns; cutting them into thin strips before cooking. You can substitute Chinese five-spice and fresh basil for the ground and fresh coriander for a variation of flavour.

Vietnamese tofu and noodle salad

An exciting layered salad combines crisp vegetables flavoured with fresh herbs, noodles and marinated grilled tofu. The tofu is best prepared several hours in advance as longer marinating will enhance the delicious flavour.

PREPARATION 20 minutes, plus at least 30 minutes marinating   COOKING 20 minutes   SERVES 4

500 g (1 lb) firm tofu, drained

3¹/₂ cups (300 g) bean sprouts, trimmed

4 cups (200 g) shredded Asian greens, such as bok choy

¹/₄ cup (15 g) chopped fresh coriander (cilantro) leaves

¹/₂ cup (7 g) chopped fresh basil

freshly squeezed juice of 2 limes

2 teaspoons caster (superfine) sugar

200 g (7 oz) snow peas (mangetout)

250 g (8 oz) dried rice stick noodles

2 tablespoons olive oil

¹/₂ cup (80 g) unsalted peanuts, chopped

¹/₂ telegraph (long) cucumber, halved lengthwise and cut into matchsticks

MARINADE

2 long green chillies, seeded and sliced

2 cloves garlic, thinly sliced

6 spring onions (scallions), thinly sliced

¹/₃ cup (80 ml) salt-reduced soy sauce

finely grated zest of 2 limes

1 teaspoon sesame oil

¹/₃ cup (80 ml) dry sherry

Each serving provides
2786 kJ, 666 kcal, 28 g protein, 29 g fat (4 g saturated fat), 66 g carbohydrate (10 g sugars), 10 g fibre, 883 mg sodium

1 Slice the tofu into 3 cm (1¹/₄ inch) thick slices and lay flat in a non-metallic dish. In a separate bowl mix together all of the marinade ingredients. Add to the tofu, turning to coat. Cover with plastic wrap and set aside for at least 30 minutes.

2 Meanwhile, combine the bean sprouts, Asian greens, coriander and basil in a large serving dish. Sprinkle with the lime juice and half of the sugar. Blanch the snow peas in a saucepan of boiling water, then refresh immediately under cold running water. Drain well and scatter over the greens.

3 Cook the noodles according to the packet instructions. Drain well, set aside and keep warm.

4 Preheat a grill (broiler) to high. Drain the tofu, pouring the marinade over the noodles and toss to coat the noodles. Drizzle half of the olive oil over the tofu and grill for 4–6 minutes, or until golden brown. Sprinkle over the remaining oil and sugar and turn the tofu slices over. Cook for a further 4 minutes, then sprinkle the peanuts over the tofu and grill for a final 2 minutes or until the peanuts are lightly toasted.

5 Arrange the noodles over the Asian greens. Slice the tofu into 2 cm (³/₄ inch) thick fingers and layer over the top of the salad with the cucumber and toasted peanuts, to serve.

ANOTHER IDEA

Instead of tofu, use thin fillets of skinless chicken breast or lean rump (round) steak. Heat the marinade for 2–3 minutes in a small bowl in the microwave before adding it to the noodles.

Thai coconut rice with seafood

This aromatic seafood and rice dish, combining the classic Thai flavourings of coconut, lime and ginger, makes a very tempting lunch. Thai jasmine rice is a naturally fragrant rice with a great texture – if you do not have any, basmati rice makes a good substitute.

PREPARATION 15 minutes   COOKING 16-18 minutes   SERVES 4

1   Put the stock in a large saucepan and bring to the boil. Add the rice, reduce the heat to low, cover, and simmer for 10-12 minutes, or until all the liquid has been absorbed and the rice is just tender.

2   Meanwhile, heat the oil in a wok or large non-stick frying pan over medium-high heat. Add the garlic, ginger and spring onions, and stir-fry for 1 minute. Add the broccoli and stir-fry for a further 2 minutes, or until just tender.

3   Add the prawns to the pan and stir-fry for 2-3 minutes, or until the prawns start to turn pink. Add the lime juice and fish sauce and stir-fry for 30 seconds, then add the coriander and season with salt and black pepper to taste.

4   Add the coconut milk to the rice and mix well to combine. Divide the rice among serving bowls, top with the stir-fried prawns and garnish with curls of coconut, if using, and lime wedges. Serve immediately.

HEALTHY EATING

Lime juice accentuates flavours, reducing the need for salt, and adds an extra boost of vitamin C to a dish. Vitamin C is a powerful antioxidant and supports the body's immune system.

2$\frac{1}{2}$ cups (625 ml) salt-reduced fish stock

1 cup (200 g) jasmine rice (Thai fragrant rice)

1 tablespoon sunflower oil

1 clove garlic, finely chopped

1 tablespoon grated fresh ginger

5 spring onions (scallions), thinly sliced

4 cups (250 g) small broccoli florets

12 raw tiger prawns (uncooked large shrimp), peeled and deveined

freshly squeezed juice of 1 lime

1 teaspoon fish sauce

3 tablespoons chopped fresh coriander (cilantro) leaves

$\frac{1}{3}$ cup (80 ml) low-fat coconut milk

lime wedges, to serve

curls of toasted fresh coconut (optional), to serve

Each serving provides
1597 kJ, 382 kcal, 20 g protein, 13 g fat
(5 g saturated fat), 45 g carbohydrate
(3 g sugars), 2 g fibre, 660 mg sodium

Fried rice with tofu and vegetables

Tossed with bright, crunchy and colourful vegetables, this fried rice is an excellent meal idea for vegetarians, with the tofu providing a boost of protein. With a tasty combination of soy, honey and ginger, this easy rice dish is a great weeknight meal idea.

PREPARATION 10 minutes, plus at least 1 hour marinating   COOKING 25 minutes   SERVES 4

1 cup (250 ml) dry white wine or
    salt-reduced chicken stock
2 tablespoons honey
1 tablespoon grated fresh ginger
1/4 cup (60 ml) salt-reduced soy sauce
2 cups (370 g) cubed firm tofu
1 cup (200 g) long-grain white rice
olive oil spray, for cooking
1 egg, beaten
2 cloves garlic, crushed
8 cups (500 g) mixed frozen stir-fry
    vegetables
5 spring onions (scallions), sliced
1/4 teaspoon black pepper

Each serving provides
1811 kJ, 433 kcal, 20 g protein, 8 g fat
(2 g saturated fat), 58 g carbohydrate
(17 g sugars), 3 g fibre, 636 mg sodium

1   Put the wine, honey, 1 teaspoon of the grated ginger and 1 tablespoon of the soy sauce in large shallow bowl with the tofu and toss to coat. Cover with plastic wrap and refrigerate for at least 1 hour, turning occasionally.

2   Put the rice into a large saucepan with 2 cups (500 ml) water. Bring to the boil, then reduce the heat, cover, and simmer for 10–15 minutes, or until all of the liquid has been absorbed and the rice is cooked. Allow to cool.

3   Grease a wok or large heavy-based frying pan with cooking spray. Add the egg and stir gently until the omelette is just set. Remove to a plate and finely slice.

4   Grease the pan again with cooking spray, add the garlic and remaining ginger to the wok and stir-fry for about 1 minute. Add the mixed vegetables, half of the spring onion, the rice, remaining soy sauce and season with the pepper. Stir-fry for 4 minutes, or until the vegetables are tender.

5   Drain the tofu and pour the marinade into a small saucepan over high heat. Bring to the boil and boil for 2 minutes, then add to the wok with the tofu. Stir-fry for about 4 minutes, or until the tofu is cooked through. Return the egg to the pan, toss to combine and sprinkle with the remaining spring onions to serve.

HEALTHY EATING

Tofu is a protein-rich food that is made from the curds of soybean milk. It is an excellent alternative to red meat as it also provides iron, selenium and omega-3 fatty acids.

Tofu noodles

PREPARATION 15 minutes, plus at least 1 hour marinating   COOKING 10 minutes   SERVES 4

2 tablespoons salt-reduced soy sauce

2 tablespoons dry sherry

2 teaspoons sesame oil

2 cloves garlic, crushed

1/2 teaspoon dried red chilli flakes

1 pinch caster (superfine) sugar

1¹/3 cups (250 g) cubed firm tofu

250 g (8 oz) soba (Japanese buckwheat noodles)

1 tablespoon vegetable oil

250 g (8 oz) bok choy, finely shredded

3/4 cup (140 g) sliced water chestnuts

2 tablespoons sesame seeds, toasted

Each serving provides
1784 kJ, 426 kcal, 18 g protein, 16 g fat
(2 g saturated fat), 44 g carbohydrate
(4 g sugars), 6 g fibre, 961 mg sodium

1   Put the soy sauce, sherry, sesame oil, garlic, chilli flakes and sugar in a bowl and stir well to combine. Add the tofu and toss to coat. Cover with plastic wrap and refrigerate for at least 1 hour.

2   Cook the soba noodles in a saucepan of boiling water for about 6 minutes, or until al dente. Drain well and set aside.

3   Heat the vegetable oil in a wok or large heavy-based frying pan over high heat. Drain the tofu, reserving the marinade, and stir-fry the tofu in the hot oil for about 30 seconds. Add the bok choy and water chestnuts and cook for a further 1 minute, stirring regularly, until the bok choy has wilted slightly.

4   Add the noodles and reserved marinade to the wok and cook for 1-2 minutes, or until heated through. Divide among serving bowls and serve with toasted sesame seeds sprinkled over the top.

Japanese red rice

PREPARATION 10 minutes, plus 9 hours soaking   COOKING 1¼ hours   SERVES 4

1   Soak the beans in water for at least 8 hours. Rinse under cold running water and drain well. Put in a saucepan with enough fresh water to cover and bring to the boil. Cook for 10 minutes, then reduce the heat and continue to simmer for about 40 minutes, or until very tender. Drain the beans and reserve the cooking liquid. Allow to cool.

2   Rinse the rice under cold running water until the water runs clear, then drain. Add the rice to the cooled adzuki bean soaking liquid and leave to soak for 1 hour.

3   Drain the rice, reserving the soaking liquid. Mix together the rice and cooked beans. Use a measuring cup to measure the combined beans and rice and add to a large saucepan. Add an equal quantity of the reserved soaking liquid, topping up with fresh water if needed. Stir in the salt. Bring to the boil, stir once, then reduce the heat to low and simmer for about 15 minutes, or until almost all the liquid has been absorbed. Stir again, cover with a tight-fitting lid and reduce the heat to its lowest setting. Leave to steam for 10 minutes.

4   Divide the rice mixture among serving bowls and use a fork to break it up. Scatter over the sesame seeds and serve.

½ cup (110 g) dried adzuki beans
1 cup (200 g) glutinous rice
½ teaspoon salt
1½ tablespoons black sesame seeds

Each serving provides
1477 kJ, 353 kcal, 11 g protein, 3 g fat
(1 g saturated fat), 69 g carbohydrate
(<1 g sugars), 5 g fibre, 379 mg sodium

HEALTHY EATING

Adzuki beans are highly nutritious. They are a great source of protein and fibre. In addition they contain a range of vitamins and minerals that are essential for a healthy low-fat diet.

Singapore noodles

These tasty noodles are stir-fried with a delicious mix of soy sauce, ginger and shaoxing rice wine and are an excellent way of using up leftover vegetables. For a quick, easy and satisfying dinner, these Singapore noodles are hard to beat.

PREPARATION 15 minutes, plus 30 minutes marinating   COOKING 10 minutes   SERVES 4

250 g (8 oz) skinless, boneless chicken breast fillets, thinly sliced

250 g (8 oz) raw prawns (uncooked shrimp), peeled and deveined

1 tablespoon shaoxing rice wine

2 cloves garlic, crushed

1/4 cup (60 ml) salt-reduced soy sauce

3 teaspoons grated fresh ginger

250 g (8 oz) rice vermicelli

2 tablespoons peanut or vegetable oil

1 tablespoon curry powder

1 red capsicum (bell pepper), halved, seeded and thinly sliced

4 spring onions (scallions), thinly sliced

1/4 cup (60 ml) salt-reduced chicken or vegetable stock

1 teaspoon sugar (optional)

fresh coriander (cilantro) sprigs, to serve

lime wedges, to serve

Each serving provides
2073 kJ, 495 kcal, 30 g protein, 14 g fat (3 g saturated fat), 57 g carbohydrate (4 g sugars), 2 g fibre, 838 mg sodium

1 Put the chicken, prawns, rice wine, garlic, 1 tablespoon of the soy sauce and 2 teaspoons of the ginger in a shallow glass or ceramic bowl and toss to coat the chicken and prawns. Cover with plastic wrap and refrigerate for 30 minutes.

2 Soak the noodles according to the packet instructions. Drain well and set aside.

3 Heat 1 tablespoon of the peanut oil in a wok or large non-stick frying pan over high heat. Add half of the chicken and prawn mixture and stir-fry for 2–3 minutes, or until just cooked through. Remove to a plate. Repeat with the remaining chicken mixture.

4 Heat the remaining oil in the clean wok. Add the curry powder and stir-fry for 30 seconds, or until aromatic. Add the capsicum, half of the spring onions and remaining ginger, and stir-fry for 1 minute, or until the onion softens. Return all of the chicken mixture to the wok, add the stock and remaining soy sauce and season with sugar, salt and freshly ground black pepper.

5 Add the noodles to the wok and toss well until the stock has been absorbed and the noodles are heated through. Garnish with fresh coriander and the remaining spring onions. Serve with lime wedges on the side.

ANOTHER IDEA

You can substitute the chicken with pork loin steak or chops or Chinese barbecued pork (char siu), which is available from Asian grocery stores. You can also add shiitake mushrooms, bean sprouts, bamboo shoots or water chestnuts.

Pad thai with chicken

PREPARATION 20 minutes, plus overnight soaking   COOKING 10 minutes   SERVES 4

250 g (8 oz) dried rice stick noodles

2 tablespoons sunflower oil

2-4 cloves garlic, crushed

1 small onion, finely chopped

1 long red or green chilli, seeded and
    finely chopped

350 g (12 oz) skinless, boneless chicken
    breast fillets, thinly sliced

2 eggs, beaten

2 cups (180 g) bean sprouts, trimmed

1 tablespoon salt-reduced soy sauce

2 tablespoons fish sauce

1 tablespoon fresh lime juice

dried red chilli flakes, to taste
    (optional)

1 bunch fresh chives, snipped, to garnish

1/4 cup (40 g) roasted peanuts,
    chopped, to garnish

lime wedges, to serve

Each serving provides
2208 kJ, 528 kcal, 29 g protein, 21 g fat
(4 g saturated fat), 55 g carbohydrate
(2 g sugars), 4 g fibre, 1300 mg sodium

1   Soak the noodles according to the packet instructions.
    Drain well and set aside.

2   Heat the sunflower oil in a wok or large non-stick frying pan
    over medium-high heat. Add the garlic, onion and chilli, and
    stir-fry for 1 minute, or until softened. Add the chicken and
    stir-fry for 2 minutes, or until lightly coloured.

3   Push the chicken to one side of the wok to make room for
    the eggs. Pour the eggs into the wok and stir gently until
    lightly scrambled. Add the noodles and 1/4 cup (60 ml) water
    to the pan, then add the bean sprouts, soy sauce, fish sauce
    and lime juice and stir-fry for 2 minutes. Season with salt
    and black pepper, to taste, and add the chilli flakes, if using.

4   Transfer to a serving dish, garnish with chives and peanuts.
    Serve immediately, with lime wedges on the side.

ANOTHER IDEA

You can substitute the chicken with pork cut into strips; cook for
5 minutes. Alternatively, you could add 250 g (8 oz) peeled and
deveined raw prawns (uncooked shrimp), adding them with the
fish sauce; cook for 3 minutes, or until they turn pink.

Noodles with plum and ginger duck

PREPARATION 15 minutes   COOKING 5 minutes   SERVES 4

1 Slice the duck breasts crosswise fairly thinly. Combine the soy sauce, rice wine and Sichuan peppercorns in a bowl. Add the duck and toss gently to coat in the marinade.

2 Cook the noodles according to the packet instructions. Drain well and set aside.

3 Heat the oil in a wok or large non-stick frying pan over high heat. Drain the duck, reserving the marinade. Add the duck to the wok and stir-fry for 1 minute. Add the spring onion, ginger and sugar snap peas and stir-fry for 1 minute. Add the reserved marinade, plum sauce and stock, reduce the heat to medium and cook for 3-4 minutes.

4 Add the noodles to the wok and toss gently to combine and heat through. Divide among bowls and serve immediately.

400 g (14 oz) skinless duck breasts
2 tablespoons salt-reduced soy sauce
2 tablespoons shaoxing rice wine or dry sherry
1 pinch ground Sichuan peppercorns or Chinese five-spice
375 g (13 oz) wok-ready Singapore or hokkien (egg) noodles
2 tablespoons olive oil
3 spring onions (scallions), sliced
1 tablespoon grated fresh ginger
300 g (10 oz) sugar snap peas or snow peas (mangetout)
4 tablespoons plum sauce
$2/3$ cup (150 ml) salt-reduced chicken or vegetable stock

Each serving provides
1850 kJ, 437 kcal, 25 g protein, 16 g fat
(4 g saturated fat), 46 g carbohydrate
(17 g sugars), 2 g fibre, 845 mg sodium

Soba noodles with smoked tofu

These days, supermarkets are stocking a wider variety of noodles. To make this tempting lunch dish, Japanese soba (hearty noodles made from buckwheat) are simmered in a soy and ginger stock with smoked tofu and an appetising mixture of vegetables.

PREPARATION 15 minutes   COOKING 15 minutes   SERVES 4

150 g (5 oz) soba (Japanese buckwheat noodles)

1 tablespoon sunflower oil

1 tablespoon grated fresh ginger

2 cloves garlic, crushed

1 red capsicum (bell pepper), halved, seeded and thinly sliced

$1/2$ cup (100 g) fresh or canned baby corn, sliced

1 cup (100 g) sliced shiitake mushrooms

4 cups (1 litre) salt-reduced vegetable stock

2 tablespoons salt-reduced soy sauce

$1/4$ cup (60 ml) dry sherry

2 spring onions (scallions), thinly sliced

$1^3/4$ cups (55 g) watercress, chopped

1 cup (90 g) bean sprouts, trimmed

$1^1/3$ cups (250 g) cubed firm smoked tofu

Each serving provides
1635 kJ, 390 kcal, 21 g protein, 12 g fat
(2 g saturated fat), 43 g carbohydrate
(11 g sugars), 4 g fibre, 2001 mg sodium

1 Cook the noodles in a saucepan of boiling water for about 6 minutes, or until al dente. Drain well and set aside.

2 Heat the sunflower oil in a separate saucepan. Add the ginger and garlic, and cook for about 1 minute, stirring often. Add the capsicum, baby corn and shiitake mushrooms, and cook for 3 minutes, stirring frequently, until the vegetables have softened.

3 Add the stock, soy sauce, sherry and 3 cups (750 ml) water to the pan and bring to the boil. Reduce the heat to low and simmer for 3 minutes, then stir in the spring onions, watercress, bean sprouts and tofu, and cook for 1 minute, or until the bean sprouts soften slightly.

4 Divide the noodles among serving bowls. Ladle the vegetables and soup over the top and serve immediately.

ANOTHER IDEA

For a tasty variation you can look out for smoked tofu that has been pre-rolled in sesame seeds and almonds. To lower the salt content in this recipe you can dilute the stock with water.

Cold sesame noodles and vegetables

PREPARATION 15 minutes   COOKING 10 minutes, plus 1 hour chilling   SERVES 6

250 g (8 oz) dried wholemeal
 (wholewheat) noodles

^{1}/$_3$ cup (10 g) fresh coriander (cilantro)
 leaves

2 tablespoons salt-reduced peanut butter

2 tablespoons salt-reduced soy sauce

2^1/$_2$ teaspoons honey

1 tablespoon rice vinegar

1 tablespoon sesame oil

2 cloves garlic, crushed

^{1}/$_4$ teaspoon cayenne pepper

2 carrots, cut into thin matchsticks

1 red capsicum (bell pepper), halved,
 seeded and thinly sliced

1 large celery stalk, thinly sliced

Each serving provides
971 kJ, 232 kcal, 8 g protein, 7 g fat
(1 g saturated fat), 33 g carbohydrate
(5 g sugars), 5 g fibre, 302 mg sodium

1   Cook the noodles according to the packet instructions. Drain well and set aside, reserving ^{1}/$_2$ cup (125 ml) of the cooking liquid.

2   Combine the coriander, peanut butter, soy sauce, honey, vinegar, sesame oil, garlic and cayenne pepper in a food processor or blender and process until well combined and smooth. Transfer to a large bowl.

3   Whisk the reserved cooking liquid into the peanut mixture. Add the noodles, carrots, capsicum and celery and toss well to combine. Cover with plastic wrap and refrigerate for at least 1 hour. Serve the noodle salad chilled.

HEALTHY EATING

The noodle cooking liquid, which carries some of the noodle's starch, is used here to 'stretch' the sauce so that it coats the noodles better. The water replaces what might otherwise be a lot of extra fat – perfect for a lighter, healthier meal.

Won ton and noodle soup

PREPARATION 20 minutes, plus 15 minutes soaking   COOKING 20 minutes   SERVES 4

1 To make the filling for the won tons, put the shiitake mushrooms in a small bowl, cover with boiling water and soak for 15 minutes, or until rehydrated. Drain well, discard the stems and thinly slice the caps. Add to a bowl with the pork, cornflour, oyster sauce, soy sauce and sesame oil and use your hands to combine well.

2 Working with one wrapper at a time, place 2 teaspoons of the pork filling in the centre of each and fold the wrapper over, pinching to seal the edges together and enclose the filling. Repeat to make 32 won tons. Set aside.

3 Cook the noodles according to the packet instructions. Drain well and divide among serving bowls. Blanch the bok choy in a saucepan of boiling water for 1 minute, or until bright green but still crunchy. Remove with a slotted spoon and divide among serving bowls

4 Put the stock, soy sauce, sesame oil and ginger in a large saucepan and bring to the boil, then cover and reduce to a simmer. Add the won tons, in batches, and cook for 3–4 minutes, or until they float to the surface. Remove with a slotted spoon and lift into the serving bowls. Ladle some of the cooking liquid into each bowl and sprinkle over the spring onions to serve.

WON TONS

1 cup (20 g) dried shiitake mushrooms
300 g (10 oz) minced (ground) pork
1 tablespoon cornflour (cornstarch)
1 tablespoon oyster sauce
3 teaspoons salt-reduced soy sauce
2 teaspoons sesame oil
32 won ton wrappers

SOUP

375 g (13 oz) wok-ready hokkien (egg) noodles
400 g (14 oz) baby bok choy, trimmed
4 cups (1 litre) salt-reduced chicken stock
2 teaspoons salt-reduced soy sauce
1½ teaspoons sesame oil
1 slice fresh ginger
3 spring onions (scallions), sliced

Each serving provides
3068 kJ, 733 kcal, 39 g protein, 11 g fat
(3 g saturated fat), 116 g carbohydrate
(7g sugars), 6 g fibre, 1700 mg sodium

Noodle-stuffed Thai omelettes

For these delectable chilli-flavoured omelettes, the eggs are whisked with cornflour (cornstarch) to give them a slightly firmer texture, suitable for folding around a tasty filling of stir-fried rice noodles and colourful pan-fried fresh vegetables.

PREPARATION 15 minutes   COOKING 15 minutes   SERVES 4

125 g (4 oz) rice vermicelli
1 tablespoon cornflour (cornstarch)
8 eggs
$1/4$–$1/2$ teaspoon crushed dried red chillies
2 tablespoons canola oil
1 teaspoon sesame oil
$1^{1}/4$ cups (115 g) sliced button or Swiss brown mushrooms
2 carrots, cut into thin matchsticks
1 green capsicum (bell pepper), halved seeded and thinly sliced
$2^{1}/4$ cups (170 g) shredded cabbage
2 tablespoons salt-reduced soy sauce
2 teaspoons white wine vinegar
2 teaspoons grated fresh ginger
1 tablespoon sesame seeds, to garnish (optional)

Each omelette provides
1590 kJ, 380 kcal, 17 g protein, 20 g fat
(4 g saturated fat), 32 g carbohydrate
(4 g sugars), 4 g fibre, 580 mg sodium

1 Soak the noodles according to the packet instructions. Drain well and set aside.

2 Put the cornflour in a large bowl with $1/4$ cup (60 ml) water and mix well until smooth. Add the eggs and whisk together until well combined. Stir in the chillies and season with a little black pepper.

3 Heat 1 teaspoon of the canola oil in a 20 cm (8 inch) non-stick frying pan over medium heat. Pour in one-quarter of the egg mixture, tipping the pan to spread out the egg in a thin, even layer. Cook for 2 minutes, or until set and golden. Remove to a plate and keep warm. Repeat with more oil and egg to make four omelettes in total.

4 Heat the remaining canola oil with the sesame oil in a wok or large non-stick frying pan. Add the mushrooms, carrots, capsicum and cabbage and stir-fry for 4–5 minutes, or until the vegetables are just tender. Add the soy sauce, vinegar, ginger and noodles. Gently toss until heated through.

5 Divide the vegetable and noodle mixture among the omelettes and fold them in half. Sprinkle with the sesame seeds, if using, and serve immediately.

HEALTHY EATING

Rice noodles contain no gluten and are therefore suitable for people with coeliac disease. Eggs are an excellent source of protein and choline, making them a wonderful addition to a healthy, low-fat vegetarian diet.

Chinese chicken noodle soup

PREPARATION 10 minutes   COOKING 5 minutes   SERVES 4

**2 cups (500 ml) salt-reduced chicken
    stock**

2 teaspoons salt-reduced soy sauce

1 teaspoon sesame oil

1 tablespoon rice vinegar

**250 g (8 oz) skinless, boneless chicken
    breast fillets, thinly sliced**

225 g (8 oz) rice vermicelli

2 cups (200 g) chopped bok choy

1 spring onion (scallion), chopped

Each serving provides
1047 kJ, 250 kcal, 21 g protein, 5 g fat
(1 g saturated fat), 28 g carbohydrate
(2 g sugars), 2 g fibre, 790 mg sodium

1 Put the stock, soy sauce, sesame oil, vinegar and 3 cups
(750 ml) water into a large saucepan and bring to the boil.
Add the chicken and cook for 2 minutes.

2 Add the noodles, bok choy and spring onion and cook for
a further 2–3 minutes, or until the noodles are cooked.
Divide among serving bowls and serve immediately.

HEALTHY EATING

Bok choy is a cruciferous vegetable and is sometimes referred
to as white cabbage. It is packed with dietary fibre and is a
rich source of vitamins.

Japanese beef with soba noodles

PREPARATION 10 minutes   COOKING 15 minutes   SERVES 4

1   Put ¼ cup (60 ml) of the soy sauce in a bowl with the garlic, cornflour and wasabi paste and mix well to combine. Add the steak and stir until well coated. Set aside.

2   Cook the noodles in a saucepan of boiling water for about 6 minutes, or until al dente. Drain well and set aside.

3   Heat 1 tablespoon of the sunflower oil in a large wok or large non-stick frying pan over high heat. Add the capsicum, spring onions and mushrooms and stir-fry for 4 minutes, or until the vegetables have softened. Remove to a plate.

4   Heat the remaining oil in the wok, add the steak and stir-fry for about 4 minutes, or until just tender. Remove to a plate.

5   Put the stock and remaining soy sauce into the wok, add the noodles, vegetables, nori and coriander. Toss well, then return the steak to the wok and toss again. Divide the noodles, vegetables and beef among serving bowls and spoon over some of the cooking liquid. Serve immediately.

½ cup (125 ml) salt-reduced dark soy sauce

2 cloves garlic, crushed

1 tablespoon cornflour (cornstarch)

1 teaspoon wasabi paste

500 g (1 lb) lean sirloin steak, trimmed and thinly sliced

300 g (10 oz) soba (Japanese buckwheat noodles)

2 tablespoons sunflower oil

1 large red capsicum (bell pepper), halved, seeded and thinly sliced

5 spring onions (scallions), sliced

1½ cups (125 g) sliced shiitake mushrooms

3 cups (750 ml) dashi stock, made with dashi powder

1 sheet nori, cut into thin strips

½ cup (15 g) chopped fresh coriander (cilantro) leaves

Each serving provides
2324 kJ, 555 kcal, 35 g protein, 18 g fat
(4 g saturated fat), 61 g carbohydrate
(5 g sugars), 4 g fibre, 1807 mg sodium

Noodles & rice

Beef noodle soup with mushrooms

Shiitake mushrooms are cultivated worldwide and are available fresh in supermarkets and most greengrocers. They have a firm, meaty texture. If you can't find them, use soaked, dried shiitake, or Swiss brown or button mushrooms instead.

PREPARATION 10 minutes   COOKING 10 minutes   SERVES 4

2 tablespoons salt-reduced soy sauce

1 tablespoon sesame oil

2 tablespoons shaoxing rice wine or dry sherry

300 g (10 oz) lean rump (round) steak, trimmed and thinly sliced

4 cups (1 litre) salt-reduced beef stock

4 spring onions (scallions), sliced

1²/₃ cups (150 g) sliced shiitake mushrooms

200 g (7 oz) baby bok choy, halved

250 g (8 oz) dried egg noodles

1 tablespoon sunflower oil

Each serving provides
1727 kJ, 413 kcal, 30 g protein, 14 g fat
(3 g saturated fat), 39 g carbohydrate
(6 g sugars), 2 g fibre, 1415 mg sodium

1   Put the soy sauce, sesame oil and shaoxing rice wine in a bowl and stir well to combine. Add the steak and toss well to coat. Set aside.

2   Put the stock in a large saucepan or flameproof casserole dish over medium-high heat. Add the spring onions, mushrooms and bok choy and simmer for 2 minutes.

3   Add the noodles to the pan and cook for 2–4 minutes, or until tender.

4   Meanwhile, heat the sunflower oil in a wok or large non-stick frying pan over high heat. Add the steak and stir-fry for 2 minutes, or until browned on both sides.

5   Add the steak and any cooking juices to the simmering stock and bring to the boil. Season with black pepper, to taste, divide among serving bowls and serve immediately.

ANOTHER IDEA

Instead of beef you can use 300 g (10 oz) skinless, boneless chicken breast fillets. If you use chicken you will need to replace the beef stock with chicken stock for a more delicate flavour.

Stir-fried rice with vegetables

Basmati rice cooks so quickly that it can be boiled and then added to a speedy stir-fry. Nuts and seeds make this a complete meal, but it's also a great side dish for grilled meats or fish.

PREPARATION 10 minutes   COOKING 15-20 minutes   SERVES 4

1 Add the rice to a saucepan of boiling water and boil for 10 minutes, or until tender. Drain well and set aside. Put the soy sauce, sherry and sesame oil in a small bowl and mix well to combine. Set aside.

2 Heat the vegetable oil in a wok or large frying pan over medium-high heat. Add the carrots and leeks and stir-fry for 2-3 minutes, or until softened. Add the cabbage, garlic and chilli, and stir-fry 2-3 minutes. Stir in the soy sauce mixture and cashew nuts. Season with salt and black pepper, to taste.

3 Add the rice to the pan and stir until heated through. Add the toasted seeds and stir well to combine. Divide the rice among serving bowls and serve immediately.

ANOTHER IDEA
You can vary the vegetables depending on what is available. Try adding strips of zucchini (courgette), eggplant (aubergine), capsicum (bell pepper) or fennel for a different flavour.

1¼ cups (250 g) basmati rice, rinsed

2 tablespoons salt-reduced soy sauce

1 tablespoon dry sherry

2 teaspoons sesame oil

2 tablespoons vegetable oil

225 g (8 oz) carrots, halved lengthwise and thinly sliced

300 g (10 oz) leeks, white part only, thinly sliced

150 g (5 oz) savoy cabbage, thinly sliced

1 clove garlic, crushed

1 long red chilli, seeded and thinly sliced, or ½ teaspoon dried red chilli flakes

½ cup (80 g) cashew nuts

½ cup (75 g) mixed seeds, toasted

Each serving provides
2496 kJ, 596 kcal, 16 g protein, 30 g fat (5 g saturated fat), 63 g carbohydrate (8 g sugars), 9 g fibre, 412 mg sodium

Poultry

Kung pao chicken

The chicken is stir-fried instead of deep-fried, reducing the fat content in this healthier version of a popular dish. It is quite spicy, with the inclusion of dried red chillies, but you can also add a fresh long red chilli for additional kick!

PREPARATION 10 minutes, plus 30 minutes marinating   COOKING 15 minutes   SERVES 4

500 g (1 lb) skinless chicken thighs, diced

2 tablespoons peanut or rice bran oil

2 cloves garlic, thinly sliced

8 dried red chillies, seeded and chopped

1 teaspoon crushed Sichuan peppercorns

2 spring onions (scallions), sliced

2 tablespoons salt-reduced soy sauce

1 tablespoon shaoxing rice wine

1 teaspoon sugar

1/3 cup (50 g) raw cashew nuts or peanuts, toasted

steamed rice, to serve

MARINADE

2 teaspoons salt-reduced soy sauce

2 teaspoons shaoxing rice wine

1 teaspoon sesame oil

1 1/2 teaspoons cornflour (cornstarch)

Each serving provides
2015 kJ, 481 kcal, 36 g protein, 30 g fat
(8 g saturated fat), 8 g carbohydrate
(4 g sugars), 2 g fibre, 765 mg sodium

1 To make the marinade, combine all of the ingredients in a shallow bowl. Add the chicken and toss to coat. Cover with plastic wrap and refrigerate for 30 minutes.

2 Heat 1 tablespoon of the peanut oil in a wok or large non-stick frying pan over high heat. Add the chicken, in two batches if necessary, and cook for 5 minutes or until just golden. Remove to a plate.

3 Heat another 1 tablespoon of the oil in the wok and add the garlic and stir-fry for 30 seconds. Add the chilli, Sichuan pepper and the white part of the spring onion and stir-fry for 1 minute, or until fragrant.

4 Combine the soy sauce, rice wine and sugar in a small bowl, then add to the chilli mixture in the wok and stir well. Add the chicken and stir-fry for about 2 minutes to heat through. Stir in the spring onion greens and cashew nuts. Remove from the heat, divide among serving bowls and serve with steamed rice.

ANOTHER IDEA

Instead of chicken thighs, you can add prawns (shrimp) or scallops to this dish. You can also add any of your favourite vegetables, such as red capsicum (bell pepper), green beans, sugarsnap peas or snow peas (mangetout).

Chicken lemongrass skewers

These chicken lemongrass skewers make an impressive starter when entertaining or can be turned into a full meal served with steamed rice or a green salad. You can also take the meat off the skewers and wrap them in crisp lettuce leaves for a unique serving idea.

PREPARATION 15 minutes   COOKING 8 minutes   SERVES 4

1 Combine the chicken, ginger, coriander, chilli, garlic, soy sauce and lime juice in a bowl and use your hands to combine and coat the chicken.

2 To make the soy ginger dipping sauce, put all of the ingredients into a small bowl and stir well to combine. Trim the ends of each lemongrass stem and cut each in half lengthwise to make 8 skewers.

3 Divide the mixture into 8 even-sized portions. Shape one portion around the middle of each lemongrass skewer, moulding it with your hands to fit – this can be done ahead and refrigerated, covered, until you are ready to cook.

4 Preheat a chargrill pan or barbecue hotplate over medium-high heat and spray the pan or hotplate with a little canola oil. Cook the skewers for 6–8 minutes, turning occasionally, until golden and cooked through. If desired, serve the skewers with the dipping sauce and lime wedges on the side.

ANOTHER IDEA

You can substitute the chicken with minced (ground) pork if you prefer. The soy ginger dipping sauce can be refrigerated in an airtight container for up to 2 weeks. You can also serve with the Asian dipping sauce on page 246 or simply with soy sauce.

600 g (1^1/$_4$ lb) minced (ground) chicken
1 tablespoon grated fresh ginger
1 cup (30 g) chopped fresh coriander (cilantro) leaves
1 long red chilli, seeded and chopped (optional)
1 clove garlic, crushed
2 tablespoons salt-reduced soy sauce
1 tablespoon fresh lime juice
4 stems lemongrass
canola oil spray, for cooking
lime wedges, to serve

SOY GINGER DIPPING SAUCE (OPTIONAL)
^{1}/$_2$ cup (125 ml) salt-reduced soy sauce
1 long red chilli, seeded and finely chopped
3 tablespoons grated fresh ginger
2 tablespoons rice vinegar

Each serving provides
1074 kJ, 257 kcal, 30 g protein, 13 g fat (4 g saturated fat), 5 g carbohydrate (<1 g sugars), <1 g fibre, 493 mg sodium

Asian chicken salad

PREPARATION 10 minutes COOKING 6 minutes SERVES 4

1 tablespoon vegetable oil

1 tablespoon grated fresh ginger

1 stem lemongrass, white part only, chopped

2 long red chillies, seeded and chopped

2 cloves garlic, chopped

500 g (1 lb) minced (ground) chicken

¼ cup (60 ml) fresh lime juice

1 tablespoon fish sauce

1 teaspoon soft brown sugar

1 red onion, thinly sliced

2 tablespoons fresh mint, chopped

1 cup (30 g) fresh coriander (cilantro) leaves

8 iceberg lettuce leaves

Each serving provides
1090 kJ, 260 kcal, 26 g protein, 15 g fat
(4 g saturated fat), 6 g carbohydrate
(3 g sugars), 3 g fibre, 577 mg sodium

1 Heat the vegetable oil in a wok or large non-stick frying pan over medium heat. Add the ginger, lemongrass, chilli and garlic and stir-fry for 1 minute. Add the chicken and stir-fry for 5 minutes, or until the chicken is cooked.

2 Remove the chicken mixture from the heat and allow to cool slightly. In a small bowl, combine the lime juice, fish sauce and sugar and pour over the chicken. Add the onion, mint, and all but a few of the coriander leaves, tossing gently to combine.

3 Divide the salad among bowls and garnish with the remaining coriander. Serve with the lettuce leaves on the side or use them to roll up the salad.

HEALTHY EATING

The leanest part of the chicken is the chicken breast, which contains less than half of the equivalent serving of red meat. Although slightly more expensive, you can ask your butcher to mince (grind) the chicken breast for you.

Teriyaki chicken skewers

PREPARATION 35 minutes, plus 30 minutes soaking and marinating   COOKING 14 minutes   SERVES 4

1 Put the chicken and half of the teriyaki marinade in a small bowl. Cover with plastic wrap and refrigerate for 30 minutes.

2 Preheat a chargrill pan or barbecue hotplate to medium-high. Thread the chicken, zucchini, capsicum, spring onions and water chestnuts onto eight 30 cm (12 inch) metal skewers. Brush with a little of the remaining teriyaki marinade.

3 Grill or barbecue the skewers for about 12-14 minutes, turning often and brushing with the marinade, until the vegetables are tender and the chicken is cooked through. Serve immediately.

ANOTHER IDEA

You can include any of your favourite vegetables to make these skewers, try small wedges of red onion, button mushrooms or even chunks of eggplant (aubergine) for a tasty variation.

500 g (1 lb) skinless chicken thighs, cut into 2.5 cm (1 inch) pieces

$1/2$ cup (125 ml) bottled teriyaki marinade

1 zucchini (courgette), quartered lengthwise and cut into 5 mm ($1/4$ inch) thick pieces

1 large red capsicum (bell pepper), cut into 2.5 cm (1 inch) squares

4 spring onions (scallions), halved

8 canned water chestnuts, rinsed and drained

Each serving provides
1135 kJ, 271 kcal, 25 g protein, 10 g fat (3 g saturated fat), 22 g carbohydrate (17 g sugars), 2 g fibre, 760 mg sodium

Sweet and sour duck salad

With ripe nectarines, green grapes, red peppery lettuce and slices of tender grilled duck, this is a particularly pretty salad. The unusual dressing complements and brings together all of the ingredients to make this a meal that is sure to impress if you are entertaining.

PREPARATION 20 minutes   COOKING 25 minutes   SERVES 4

1¼ cups (250 g) mixed basmati and
   wild rice
4 x 125 g (4 oz) skinless, boneless duck
   breasts
2 teaspoons olive oil
2¾ cups (85 g) watercress leaves
1 cup (180 g) seedless green grapes,
   halved
4 spring onions (scallions), thinly sliced
3 celery stalks, thinly sliced
4 nectarines
8 radicchio leaves or other red salad
   leaves
¼ cup (30 g) pepitas (pumpkin seeds),
   toasted

SWEET AND SOUR DRESSING
1 teaspoon grated fresh ginger
1 clove garlic, finely chopped
1 tablespoon apricot jam
2 teaspoons raspberry vinegar or white
   wine vinegar
2 tablespoons hazelnut oil

Each serving provides
2492 kJ, 595 kcal, 37 g protein, 25 g fat
(5 g saturated fat), 75 g carbohydrate
(24 g sugars), 7 g fibre, 50 mg sodium

1   Cook the rice in a saucepan of boiling water for about 20 minutes, or until tender. Drain well, then transfer to a bowl and allow to cool.

2   Heat a chargrill pan over medium-high heat. Trim the duck breasts of excess fat and brush the olive oil over to coat on both sides. Cook for 3 minutes on each side (the meat will be rare, so cook longer if you prefer it well done). Remove from the heat and set aside to cool.

3   To make the sweet and sour dressing, put the ginger, garlic, apricot jam, vinegar and hazelnut oil in a small bowl and stir to combine. Season with pepper, to taste. Set aside.

4   Chop half of the watercress and stir through the rice. Add the grapes, spring onions and celery, drizzle over half of the dressing and toss gently to combine.

5   Thinly slice the duck breasts and nectarines. Arrange the radicchio and reserved watercress leaves on serving plates and divide the rice salad among them. Arrange the duck and nectarine slices on top, drizzle with the remaining dressing and sprinkle with the pepitas, to serve.

HEALTHY EATING
Nectarines are high in vitamin C, beta-carotene and potassium. They are high in fibre, low in kilojoules and are virtually fat-free, making them a wonderful addition to any meal.

Chicken, lychee and plum salad

This chicken salad has an Asian twist. Grilled chicken is tossed with oranges, green vegetables and lychees and is then crowned with a drizzle of creamy peanut dressing. This dish is great for your heart health and your waistline!

PREPARATION 20 minutes   COOKING 10 minutes   SERVES 4

1   Put the lettuce, snow peas, lychees, orange, plum and spring onions in a large bowl and toss to combine.

2   Grease a wok or large non-stick frying pan with cooking spray and set over medium-high heat. Add the chicken breast fillets and cook for about 4 minutes on each side, or until cooked through. Remove from the heat and allow to cool slightly, then cut into thin slices on the diagonal.

3   To make the creamy peanut dressing, whisk the mayonnaise, peanut butter and garlic in a small bowl. Add the chicken strips to the salad and just before serving, drizzle over the dressing and toss to coat.

ANOTHER IDEA
This salad works with many types of cooked lean meat and seafood. In place of the chicken, cook the same amount of boneless lamb, turkey breast, pork fillet, sirloin steak or you can even add raw tiger prawns (uncooked large shrimp).

500 g (1 lb) cos (romaine) lettuce, finely shredded

1^1/$_2$ cups (150 g) trimmed and sliced snow peas (mangetout)

3 cups (565 g) canned lychees, drained and halved

1 large navel orange, peeled, white pith removed and cut into sections

1 red plum, halved, stone removed and sliced

4 spring onions (scallions), thinly sliced

olive oil spray, for cooking

375 g (13 oz) skinless, boneless chicken breast fillets

CREAMY PEANUT DRESSING

^{1}/$_3$ cup (80 ml) low-fat mayonnaise

3 tablespoons salt-reduced smooth peanut butter

1 clove garlic, finely chopped

Each serving provides
1808 kJ, 432 kcal, 29 g protein, 17 g fat
(4 g saturated fat), 42 g carbohydrate
(38 g sugars), 7 g fibre, 433 mg sodium

Chicken and soba noodle salad

PREPARATION 20 minutes COOKING 15 minutes SERVES 4

³/4 cup (180 ml) salt-reduced chicken stock

2 cloves garlic, crushed

¹/2 teaspoon ground ginger

¹/4 teaspoon dried crushed chilli

375 g (13 oz) skinless, boneless chicken breast fillets

300 g (10 oz) soba (Japanese buckwheat noodles)

250 g (8 oz) green beans, halved

2 carrots, cut into matchsticks

1¹/2 tablespoons dark brown sugar

3 teaspoons salt-reduced soy sauce

3 teaspoons vegetable oil

2 cups (150 g) shredded cabbage

Each serving provides
2007 kJ, 479 kcal, 32 g protein, 10 g fat
(2 g saturated fat), 63 g carbohydrate
(9 g sugars), 7 g fibre, 1022 mg sodium

1 Put the stock, garlic, ginger and chilli in a wok or large non-stick frying pan over medium–high heat and bring to the boil. Reduce the heat to medium–low, add the chicken, cover and simmer for 10 minutes, or until the chicken is cooked through. Remove the chicken to a plate, reserving the cooking liquid. Shred the chicken meat into small pieces.

2 Cook the noodles in a saucepan of boiling water for 6 minutes, or until al dente. Drain well and set aside.

3 Blanch the beans and carrots in a saucepan of boiling water for 1 minute, or until tender. Refresh immediately in cold water and drain well.

4 Whisk together the sugar, soy sauce, vegetable oil and the reserved cooking liquid in a large bowl. Add the shredded chicken, noodles, beans, carrots and the cabbage, tossing to combine. Serve at room temperature, or chilled.

Stir-fried chicken with coconut milk

PREPARATION 20 minutes   COOKING 8-10 minutes   SERVES 4

1. Put the lime zest and juice in a bowl with the coconut milk, soy sauce, ginger, sugar, cornflour and curry paste, if using, and mix well to combine. Set aside.

2. Heat 1 tablespoon of the vegetable oil in a wok or large non-stick frying pan over high heat. Add the onion and garlic and stir-fry for 2 minutes, or until the onion softens. Add the broccoli florets and stalks, and the mushrooms, and stir-fry for a further 2 minutes. Remove to a bowl.

3. Heat the remaining oil in the wok. Add the chicken and stir-fry for 2 minutes, or until lightly golden. Add the coconut milk mixture, return the vegetables to the pan and stir-fry for 1 minute, or until the sauce thickens slightly. Cover and simmer for 2 minutes, or until the chicken is cooked through and the vegetables are just tender. Scatter with the basil, toss together briefly, and serve immediately.

finely grated zest of 1 lime
1 tablespoon fresh lime juice
$^2/_3$ cup (150 ml) low-fat coconut milk
1 tablespoon salt-reduced soy sauce
1 tablespoon grated fresh ginger
1 tablespoon soft brown sugar
1 teaspoon cornflour (cornstarch)
$^1/_2$ teaspoon green curry paste (optional) (see page 248)
2 tablespoons vegetable oil
1 onion, halved and sliced
6 cloves garlic, crushed
1 head broccoli, cut into small florets, stalks thinly sliced
250 g (8 oz) button mushrooms, halved
375 g (13 oz) skinless, boneless chicken breast or thigh fillets, cut into thin strips
$^1/_4$ cup (7 g) fresh basil, chopped

Each serving provides
1554 kJ, 371 kcal, 31 g protein, 20 g fat
(7 g saturated fat), 11 g carbohydrate
(6 g sugars), 9 g fibre, 305 mg sodium

Chicken and broccoli stir-fry

There's no cooking method that's faster or easier than stir-frying. You'll love blending these fresh green vegetables with chicken (or with meat, fish or tofu) for a fast stir-fry, and then creating the sauce in the wok for a healthy meal.

PREPARATION 10 minutes   COOKING 10 minutes   SERVES 4

3 teaspoons peanut oil

3 spring onions (scallions), thinly sliced

350 g (12 oz) skinless, boneless chicken breast fillets, cut into 1 cm ($1/2$ inch) pieces

680 g ($1^1/_2$ lb) broccoli, cut into small florets

1 cup (150 g) diced red capsicum (bell pepper)

$1/2$ cup (125 ml) salt-reduced chicken stock

$1/2$ teaspoon finely grated lemon zest

$1/2$ teaspoon salt

1 teaspoon cornflour (cornstarch) mixed with 1 tablespoon water

1 tablespoon olive oil

2 tablespoons chopped fresh basil

250 g (8 oz) orzo (rice-shaped pasta) or other small soup pasta

Each serving provides
1965 kJ, 470 kcal, 32 g protein, 14 g fat (3 g saturated fat), 53 g carbohydrate (3 g sugars), 8 g fibre, 555 mg sodium

1   Heat 2 teaspoons of the peanut oil in a wok or large non-stick frying pan over medium heat. Add the spring onion and cook for 1 minute, or until wilted. Add the chicken and cook for 3 minutes, or until no longer pink. Add the remaining oil and the broccoli, and continue cooking for 2 minutes.

2   Add the capsicum, stock, lemon zest and salt to the wok with $1/2$ cup (125 ml) water and bring to the boil. Reduce the heat to low and simmer for 2 minutes, or until the chicken and broccoli are cooked through.

3   Add the cornflour mixture, olive oil and basil to the wok and stir-fry for 1 minute, or until the sauce thickens slightly. Remove from the heat and keep warm.

4   Cook the orzo following the packet instructions. Drain well and divide among serving plates. Serve with the chicken and broccoli stir-fry over the top.

ANOTHER IDEA

You can replace the broccoli in this dish with any fresh Asian green vegetables, such as bok choy, Chinese broccoli (gai larn) or Chinese cabbage (wombok), depending on your preference.

Chicken satay stir-fry

PREPARATION 15 minutes   COOKING 15 minutes   Serves 4

¹/₄ cup (60 g) salt-reduced smooth
    peanut butter
¹/₃ cup (80 ml) low-fat coconut milk
2 tablespoons salt-reduced chicken stock
finely grated zest of 1 lemon
1 tablespoon vegetable oil
2 cloves garlic, crushed
1 long red chilli, seeded and chopped
350 g (12 oz) skinless, boneless chicken
    breast fillets, thinly sliced
1 tablespoon Chinese five-spice
1 red capsicum (bell pepper), halved,
    seeded and sliced
2 carrots, cut into thin matchsticks
2 cups (180 g) sliced button mushrooms
2 tablespoons chopped fresh coriander
    (cilantro) leaves

Each serving provides
1326 kJ, 317 kcal, 25 g protein, 20 g fat
(6 g saturated fat), 9 g carbohydrate
(5 g sugars), 3 g fibre, 221 mg sodium

1 In a small bowl, whisk together the peanut butter, coconut milk, stock and lemon zest until well combined. Set aside.

2 Heat the vegetable oil in a wok or large non-stick frying pan over high heat. Add the garlic and chilli and stir-fry for 30 seconds to release the flavours.

3 Add the chicken and Chinese five-spice to the wok and stir-fry for 3–4 minutes, or until the chicken is coloured all over. Add the capsicum, carrot and mushroom and stir-fry for 2–3 minutes, or until slightly softened.

4 Pour the peanut butter mixture into the wok and stir-fry for a further 2–3 minutes, or until the chicken is cooked through and tender. Remove from the heat, stir in the coriander and serve immediately.

HEALTHY EATING
Red chillies are a great source of beta-carotene and vitamin C. You can spice this dish up a little by leaving the seeds in the chilli – chillies contain most of their heat in the seeds and membrane.

Poultry

92

Chicken noodle soup

PREPARATION 20 minutes   COOKING 20 minutes   SERVES 4

1   Put the chicken stock, lemongrass, ginger, chilli, garlic and 2 cups (500 ml) water into a large saucepan and bring to the boil. Add the chicken, reduce the heat and simmer for about 15 minutes, or until the chicken is cooked through. Remove the chicken to a plate to cool slightly, reserving the stock.

2   Break or cut the noodles into the hot stock, then add the baby corn, mushrooms, soy sauce and coconut milk. Bring back to a simmer and cook for 3 minutes.

3   Meanwhile, finely shred the chicken into small pieces. Stir the chicken into the soup with the lime zest and juice and the bok choy and simmer for 2 minutes, or until the bok choy has wilted.

4   Divide the soup among serving bowls and scatter with the spring onions and coriander leaves. Serve immediately.

4 cups (1 litre) salt-reduced chicken stock

2 stems lemongrass, white part only, finely chopped

2 teaspoons grated fresh ginger

1 long red chilli, seeded and finely chopped

2 cloves garlic, finely chopped

400 g (14 oz) skinless, boneless chicken breast fillets

150 g (5 oz) dried rice stick noodles

1 cup (180 g) sliced fresh or canned baby corn

1^2/$_3$ cups (150 g) sliced button mushrooms

1 tablespoon salt-reduced soy sauce

1 cup (250 ml) low-fat coconut milk

finely grated zest of 1 lime

freshly squeezed juice of 1 lime

2^2/$_3$ cups (200 g) sliced bok choy

3 spring onions (scallions), thinly sliced

^{1}/$_4$ cup (7 g) fresh coriander (cilantro) leaves, roughly chopped

Each serving provides
1742 kJ, 416 kcal, 29 g protein, 13 g fat (8 g saturated fat), 44 g carbohydrate (6 g sugars), 4 g fibre, 960 mg sodium

Poultry

93

Warm sesame chicken salad

Strips of chicken in a crisp coating of sesame seeds, breadcrumbs and cornflakes are served on a crunchy vegetable salad dressed with a fresh herb vinaigrette. A little chilli powder in the coating gives the salad a bit of a spicy kick.

PREPARATION 15 minutes   COOKING 20 minutes   SERVES 4

1   Preheat the oven to 200°C (400°F/Gas 6). Slice each chicken breast in half horizontally, then cut lengthwise into large strips.

2   Place the breadcrumbs, cornflakes, sesame seeds and chilli powder in a plastic bag and shake to mix well. Dip the chicken strips, one at a time, into the egg mixture, then drop into the plastic bag. When a few pieces of chicken are in the bag, shake to coat evenly with the sesame seed mixture. As the chicken strips are coated, transfer to a non-stick baking tray, arranging the chicken in a single layer.

3   Bake the chicken strips for 15-20 minutes, turning the pieces over halfway through cooking.

4   Meanwhile, to make the herb dressing, place all of the ingredients in a small bowl and stir well to combine. Season with pepper, to taste. Put the cabbage, chicory and witlof leaves in a large bowl and toss to combine. Pour over the dressing and toss again to coat.

5   Divide the salad among serving plates and pile the cooked chicken pieces on top. Garnish with the extra sesame seeds, and serve immediately.

HEALTHY EATING

Cabbage belongs to a family of vegetables that contains a number of different phytochemicals. It is also a good source of vitamin C and folate.

500 g (1 lb) skinless, boneless chicken breast fillets
1 cup (80 g) fresh wholemeal (wholewheat) breadcrumbs
1 cup (50 g) lightly crushed cornflakes
1 tablespoon sesame seeds, plus extra to garnish
1 teaspoon chilli powder, or to taste
2 eggs, lightly beaten
1/4 cabbage, finely shredded
1/2 chicory (curly endive), leaves separated
2 heads witlof (Belgian endive), leaves separated

HERB DRESSING

1 tablespoon chopped fresh flat-leaf parsley
1 tablespoon chopped fresh oregano
1 tablespoon chopped fresh tarragon
1 tablespoon white wine vinegar
1/3 cup (80 ml) olive oil
1 teaspoon honey

Each serving provides
2190 kJ, 523 kcal, 36 g protein, 30 g fat (6 g saturated fat), 26 g carbohydrate (5 g sugars), 5 g fibre, 339 mg sodium

Teriyaki grilled poussin

Once spatchcocked (split open and flattened), poussins can be quickly grilled, each bird providing a single serving. Here they are basted with a Japanese-style mixture made with fresh ginger, soy sauce and sesame oil. Serve with rice and steamed green vegetables.

PREPARATION 15 minutes, plus 30 minutes marinating   COOKING 30 minutes   SERVES 2

2 x 400 g (14 oz) poussins (baby chickens)

2 cloves garlic, crushed

1 tablespoon grated fresh ginger

1 tablespoon honey

2 teaspoons sesame oil

1¹/₂ tablespoons bottled teriyaki marinade

2 tablespoons salt-reduced soy sauce

¹/₂ teaspoon chopped long red chilli, or to taste, plus extra whole chillies, to garnish (optional)

Each serving provides
2007 kJ, 480 kcal, 55 g protein, 18 g fat (5 g saturated fat), 23 g carbohydrate (20 g sugars), 1 g fibre, 1195 mg sodium

1 To spatchcock the poussins, use a knife or poultry shears to cut up one side of the backbone, then cut out the backbone altogether. Open out each bird on a chopping board, skin side up, and press down firmly with the palm of your hand. Cut off the wing tips and knuckles to make the birds a neater shape, then carefully remove the skin. Secure each bird in a flat position with a long metal skewer, pushing it through crosswise from the meaty part of one drumstick to the other. Place the birds in a large shallow dish or roasting pan.

2 Put the garlic, ginger, honey, sesame oil, teriyaki marinade, soy sauce and chilli in a bowl and mix well to combine. Pour over the poussins, turning so they are well coated on both sides. Set aside to marinate for at least 30 minutes.

3 Preheat the grill (broiler) to high. Place the poussins on the grill rack, skin side down, and cook for about 20 minutes, basting frequently with the teriyaki mixture and turning over after 10 minutes, or until cooked through. Test by piercing the thigh with the tip of a knife; the juices that run out should be clear. Remove the skewers.

4 Meanwhile, make the chillies into 'flowers', if using, by slicing one end of each chilli into fine 'petals'. Serve the poussins hot with steamed rice and garnished with the chilli flowers.

ANOTHER IDEA

You can use 4 skinless, boneless chicken breast fillets instead of the poussins, to serve 4 people. Double the ingredients for the teriyaki baste, except the sesame oil, and grill for 10-12 minutes.

Spicy stir-fried duck

Lightly dusted with Chinese five-spice, this tasty duck breast is stir-fried with a little honey, pear and fresh Asian greens to make a modern Asian lunch or dinner. It can be served as part of a shared meal with your favourite noodles or steamed rice on the side.

PREPARATION 15 minutes   COOKING 10 minutes   SERVES 4

1   Cut the duck breasts into thin strips and sprinkle over the five-spice to coat. Set aside.

2   Heat the sunflower oil in a wok or heavy-based frying pan over high heat and swirl to coat the base and side. Add the duck pieces and stir-fry for 2 minutes, then add the onions and celery and stir-fry for 3 minutes, or until softened. Add the pear and water chestnuts and stir well to combine.

3   Add the honey, vinegar and soy sauce to the wok and heat through. When the liquid is bubbling, reduce the heat to low and simmer for a further 2 minutes.

4   Increase the heat to high, then add the bok choy and bean sprouts, and stir-fry for 1 minute, or until the bok choy has just wilted.

5   Divide the duck and vegetables among serving plates and serve immediately, garnished with celery leaves.

HEALTHY EATING

Bean sprouts are rich in vitamin C and several of the B vitamins; they also provide some potassium. Adding them at the last minute preserves as much of their vitamin C content as possible

400 g (14 oz) skinless, boneless duck breasts, trimmed of fat

2 teaspoons Chinese five-spice

2 tablespoons sunflower oil

4 small onions, thinly sliced

4 small celery stalks, thinly sliced, plus a few leaves, to garnish

1 firm pear, peeled, cored and diced

$1^1/_2$ cups (230 g) sliced canned water chestnuts

1 tablespoon honey

$^1/_4$ cup (60 ml) rice vinegar or sherry vinegar

1 tablespoon salt-reduced soy sauce

$2^2/_3$ cups (200 g) shredded bok choy

$1^1/_2$ cups (135 g) bean sprouts, trimmed

Each serving provides
1304 kJ, 312 kcal, 21 g protein, 16 g fat (3 g saturated fat), 20 g carbohydrate (15 g sugars), 4 g fibre, 219 mg sodium

Poultry

Chicken with broccoli and tomato

This satisfying chicken stir-fry, flavoured simply with soy sauce, garlic and ginger, is full of colour and packed with vitamins. It makes an easy meal idea and can be served on its own or with buckwheat noodles or steamed rice.

PREPARATION 10 minutes   COOKING 10 minutes   SERVES 4

2 teaspoons canola oil

500 g (1 lb) skinless, boneless chicken breast fillets, cut into 3 cm (1¹/₄ inch) cubes

1 tablespoon salt-reduced soy sauce

2 cloves garlic, crushed

1 teaspoon grated fresh ginger

3 cups (180 g) small broccoli florets

1 cup (250 ml) salt-reduced chicken stock

1 tablespoon cornflour (cornstarch)

4 firm, ripe roma (plum) tomatoes, quartered lengthwise

Each serving provides
1024 kJ, 245 kcal, 32 g protein, 10 g fat (2 g saturated fat), 7 g carbohydrate (4 g sugars), 4 g fibre, 438 mg sodium

1 Heat the canola oil in a wok or large non-stick frying pan over high heat. Add the chicken and stir-fry for 3 minutes, then add the soy sauce, garlic and ginger and stir well.

2 Add the broccoli to the wok, then slowly add ¹/₂ cup (125 ml) of the stock. Cover and cook for 2–3 minutes, or until the broccoli is just tender.

3 Meanwhile, mix the cornflour into the remaining stock until it dissolves. Add the cornflour mixture and tomato to the pan and simmer for 2 minutes, or until the sauce thickens. Divide among serving bowls and serve immediately.

ANOTHER IDEA

You can substitute lean slices of beef or pork loin for the chicken and red or yellow capsicum (bell pepper) for the tomato. If you use capsicum, add to the frying pan with the broccoli.

Chicken salad with tahini dressing

The ingredients for this salad are presented individually on a platter rather than being mixed together, with a simple tahini-based dressing so everyone can help themselves. Careful and neat slicing of the vegetables will improve the overall presentation of this dish.

PREPARATION 25 minutes   COOKING 15 minutes   SERVES 4

1   Place the chicken breast fillets on a heatproof plate in a steamer over a saucepan of boiling water. Sprinkle with the mirin or sake and season with salt and black pepper. Cover and steam for 10–12 minutes, or until the chicken is cooked through. Set aside to cool.

2   To make the tahini dressing, mix together all of the ingredients, except the chilli powder, in a bowl. Drain the cooking juices from the chicken and add enough water to measure 1/3 cup (80 ml). Add to the dressing, mixing well to combine. Add a little more lemon juice, if needed. Pour into a serving bowl and sprinkle with chilli powder, if using.

3   To make the salad, cut the cucumber, carrots and red capsicum into fine strips of similar length, about 5 cm (2 inches) each. Arrange the lettuce leaves at one end of a large platter. Scatter with the chopped basil and mint. Cut the chicken into strips and place on the lettuce. Arrange all of the other salad ingredients on the platter. Serve with the dressing on the side for guests to help themselves.

HEALTHY EATING

Typical of most Asian cooking, this dish is composed of only a small amount of meat per person, and plenty of raw vegetables to fill you up. Raw vegetables retain all of the their health benefits and are also very low in fat.

300 g (10 oz) skinless, boneless chicken breast fillets

1 tablespoon mirin or sake

10 cm (4 inch) piece telegraph (long) cucumber

2 carrots

1 red capsicum (bell pepper), seeded

2 baby cos lettuces, leaves separated

1/2 cup (10 g) fresh basil leaves, chopped

1/2 cup (6 g) fresh mint leaves, chopped

8 spring onions (scallions), halved lengthwise

1 1/4 cups (115 g) sliced button mushrooms

TAHINI DRESSING

2 tablespoons tahini

1 clove garlic, crushed

1 tablespoon salt-reduced soy sauce

2 teaspoons fresh lemon juice, or to taste

chilli powder, to garnish (optional)

Each serving provides
882 kJ, 210 kcal, 22 g protein, 10 g fat (2 g saturated fat), 6 g carbohydrate (6 g sugars), 5 g fibre, 267 mg sodium

Teriyaki chicken with vegetables

You can marinate the chicken ahead of time, and then all you have to do before serving is briefly cook it with the vegetables. If you like, serve with steamed rice to make it a complete meal.

PREPARATION 10 minutes, plus at least 1 hour marinating   COOKING 10-12 minutes   SERVES 4

500 g (1 lb) skinless, boneless chicken breast fillets, thickly sliced

150 g (5 oz) shiitake mushrooms, halved

1 teaspoon grated fresh ginger

200 g (7 oz) snow peas (mangetout)

2^1/$_4$ cups (200 g) bean sprouts, trimmed

1 cup (250 g) sliced canned bamboo shoots

1 cup (150 g) frozen peas

TERIYAKI MARINADE

2 cloves garlic, crushed

2 tablespoons dry sherry

1 tablespoon salt-reduced soy sauce

1 tablespoon sesame oil

2 teaspoons vegetable oil

1 teaspoon rice vinegar

^{1}/$_2$ teaspoon caster (superfine) sugar

Each serving provides
1308 kJ, 312 kcal, 33 g protein, 14 g fat
(3 g saturated fat), 9 g carbohydrate
(6 g sugars), 4 g fibre, 267 mg sodium

1 To make the teriyaki marinade, put all of the ingredients in a large bowl and stir well to combine. Add the chicken strips and gently toss to coat. Cover with plastic wrap and refrigerate for at least 1 hour.

2 Heat a wok or large non-stick frying pan over medium heat. Add the chicken and marinade and cook for 4 minutes, stirring occasionally. Remove the chicken to a plate, reserving the marinade in the wok. Cover the chicken to keep warm.

3 Add the mushrooms and ginger to the wok and cook for about 2 minutes over high heat, stirring frequently.

4 Add the snow peas to the wok and stir-fry for 1 minute, then add the bean sprouts and stir-fry for a further 1 minute. Stir in the bamboo shoots and peas, cover, and cook gently for 2 minutes. Return the chicken to the pan and reheat for 1-2 minutes before serving.

HEALTHY EATING

Both green peas and snow peas are terrifically good for you. They contain a multitude of vitamins and minerals which deliver a much-needed balance to the chicken protein.

Chicken skewers with peanut sauce

PREPARATION 20 minutes, plus 30 minutes soaking   COOKING 5 minutes   SERVES 4

2 tablespoons mirin

2 teaspoons sesame oil

$1/2$ teaspoon dried crushed chilli

2 teaspoons sugar

2 telegraph (long) cucumbers, diced

1 red capsicum (bell pepper), seeded and diced

500 g (1 lb) skinless, boneless chicken breast fillets, cut into cubes

$1/2$ teaspoon ground coriander

2 cloves garlic, crushed

$1/2$ cup (80 g) peanuts, roasted

$1/3$ cup (10 g) fresh coriander (cilantro) leaves

$1/2$ cup (125 ml) salt-reduced chicken stock

2 tablespoons fresh lime juice

lemon wedges, to serve

Each serving provides
1452 kJ, 347 kcal, 35 g protein, 19 g fat
(4 g saturated fat), 8 g carbohydrate
(7 g sugars), 4 g fibre, 260 mg sodium

1 In a bowl, whisk together the mirin, sesame oil, chilli and 1 teaspoon of the sugar. Add the cucumbers and capsicum and toss to combine. Refrigerate until needed.

2 Preheat a chargrill pan or barbecue hotplate to medium. Soak 8 wooden skewers in water for 30 minutes to prevent them from burning during cooking. Season the chicken with salt and black pepper, add the ground coriander and toss well to coat. Set aside until needed.

3 Put the remaining sugar, garlic, peanuts, coriander, stock and lime juice in a food processor and process until well combined and smooth. Set aside.

4 Thread the chicken pieces onto the skewers. Grill the chicken skewers for about 5 minutes, turning once, until the chicken is cooked through.

5 Serve the skewers with the cucumber salad and lemon wedges on the side, with the peanut sauce passed separately in a smaller dish.

Chinese chicken soup

PREPARATION 15 minutes   COOKING 10 minutes   SERVES 4

1   Put the chicken, soy sauce and sesame oil in a bowl and toss to coat the chicken. Set aside for 5 minutes.

2   Put the stock, garlic and Chinese five-spice in a large saucepan and bring to the boil.

3   Add the chicken and marinade to the pan together with the carrot. Reduce the heat to medium-low and simmer for 5 minutes. Stir in the spinach and spring onions and simmer for a further 1 minute until the spinach has wilted. Divide among serving bowls and serve immediately.

ANOTHER IDEA

To make a vegetarian version of this soup, simply replace the chicken with $1^1/_3$ cups (250 g) firm cubed tofu and replace the chicken stock with vegetable stock. You can also replace the spinach with any other Asian greens or broccoli florets.

250 g (8 oz) skinless, boneless, chicken breast fillets, cut into 3 cm ($1^1/_4$ inch) cubes

2 teaspoons salt-reduced soy sauce

$^1/_2$ teaspoon sesame oil

2 cups (500 ml) salt-reduced chicken stock

2 large cloves garlic, finely chopped

$^1/_4$ teaspoon Chinese five-spice

1 small carrot, thinly sliced

2 cups (125 g) chopped spinach leaves, thick stems removed

2 spring onions (scallions), thinly sliced

Each serving provides
491 kJ, 117 kcal, 16 g protein, 4 g fat
(1 g saturated fat), 3 g carbohydrate
(3 g sugars), 2 g fibre, 535 mg sodium

Chicken hotpot

This dish is a fun way to eat and entertain! Ideally, this Chinese fondue is cooked in a large pot on a portable burner in the middle of the table so guests can cook their own. Alternatively, everything can be cooked at once on the stovetop and served in individual bowls.

PREPARATION 15 minutes COOKING 10 minutes SERVES 4

1 Soak the noodles according to the packet instructions. Drain well and arrange on a platter with the Chinese cabbage, carrot, mushrooms, spring onions and bok choy.

2 To make the ponzu dipping sauce, combine all of the ingredients in a bowl with ¼ cup (60 ml) water. Set aside.

3 Put the stock into a wok or large saucepan and bring to the boil. Reduce the heat to low, add the chicken and simmer for 2–3 minutes, or until nearly cooked through. Add the tofu and cook for 2–3 minutes, or until golden. Add a selection of the vegetables with some noodles and cook 1–2 minutes, or until tender. Remove all the ingredients from the wok a few at a time, then dip into the ponzu dipping sauce. Once all of the ingredients are eaten, drink any remaining stock as a soup or with any remaining noodles or even rice.

ANOTHER IDEA
Many other ingredients can be added to this dish, such as skinless, boneless firm white fish fillets, squid tubes, scallops, mussels, enoki or Swiss brown mushrooms, leeks, green beans, broccolini or any Asian greens.

100 g (3½ oz) rice vermicelli

6 Chinese cabbage (wombok) leaves, chopped

1 small carrot, finely sliced

12 small shiitake or oyster mushrooms, halved

4 spring onions (scallions), cut into short lengths

250 g (8 oz) baby bok choy, chopped

6 cups (1.5 litres) dashi, chicken or vegetable stock

400 g (14 oz) skinless, boneless chicken breast fillets, thinly sliced

300 g (10 oz) firm tofu, cut into cubes

PONZU DIPPING SAUCE

¼ cup (60 ml) fresh lemon juice

¼ cup (60 ml) salt-reduced shoyu (Japanese soy sauce)

2 spring onions (scallions), finely sliced

Each serving provides
1394 kJ, 333 kcal, 33 g protein, 11 g fat (3 g saturated fat), 24 g carbohydrate (4 g sugars), 3 g fibre, 884 mg sodium

Chicken and cashew stir-fry

PREPARATION 15 minutes   COOKING 10 minutes   SERVES 4

3 cups (180 g) small broccoli florets

375 g (13 oz) skinless chicken thighs, cut into 2 cm (³/₄ inch) cubes

3 teaspoons salt-reduced soy sauce

3 teaspoons dry sherry

2 teaspoons vegetable oil

3 teaspoons grated fresh ginger

3 cloves garlic, crushed

1 red capsicum (bell pepper), halved, seeded and chopped

¹/₂ cup (125 ml) salt-reduced chicken stock

2 tablespoons chilli sauce

2 teaspoons cornflour (cornstarch)

2 spring onions (scallions), sliced

¹/₄ cup (40 g) cashew nuts, chopped

Each serving provides
1069 kJ, 255 kcal, 23 g protein, 15 g fat
(3 g saturated fat), 8 g carbohydrate
(4 g sugars), 4 g fibre, 536 mg sodium

1   Blanch the broccoli in a saucepan of boiling water for 1 minute, or until just tender. Refresh immediately in cold water and set aside. Combine the chicken, soy sauce and sherry in a bowl and toss to coat.

2   Heat the vegetable oil in a wok or large non-stick frying pan. Add the chicken and stir-fry for 3 minutes; remove to a plate. Add the ginger and garlic to the wok and stir-fry for about 30 seconds, then add the broccoli and capsicum and stir-fry for 2 minutes, or until the capsicum has softened.

3   Add the stock and chilli sauce and bring to the boil. Combine the cornflour with 1 tablespoon water; add to the pan and stir for 1 minute, or until slightly thickened. Return the chicken to the pan; add the spring onions and cook for 1 minute. Stir in the cashew nuts just before serving.

HEALTHY EATING
Cashew nuts are a good source of monounsaturated fats, which can help lower blood cholesterol. They also contain copper and magnesium, making them a healthy addition to any meal.

Poultry

Chinese walnut chicken

PREPARATION 15 minutes   COOKING 20 minutes   SERVES 4

1 Heat 1 teaspoon of the vegetable oil in a wok or large non-stick frying pan over medium heat. Add 1$^1/_2$ tablespoons of the sugar, stirring until it dissolves. Add the walnuts and stir-fry for 7 minutes, or until they are lightly toasted. Remove to a plate.

2 Heat the remaining vegetable oil in the wok over medium-high heat. Add the capsicum and cook for 2 minutes, or until tender. Add the spring onions, garlic and ginger and cook for 2 minutes, then add the chicken and cook for 4 minutes.

3 Combine the stock, soy sauce, sesame oil and the remaining sugar in a small bowl. Add the cornflour and stir well to combine. Add to the frying pan, bring to the boil, then cook for 3 minutes, or until the sauce is slightly thickened and the chicken is cooked through. Stir in the walnuts, then divide among serving bowls and serve immediately.

3 teaspoons vegetable oil

2 tablespoons sugar

1 cup (100 g) walnuts

1 red capsicum (bell pepper), halved, seeded and thinly sliced

4 spring onions (scallions), sliced

2 cloves garlic, crushed

1 tablespoon grated fresh ginger

500 g (1 lb) skinless, boneless chicken breast fillets, cut into 3 cm (1$^1/_4$ inch) cubes

1 cup (250 ml) salt-reduced chicken stock

3 teaspoons salt-reduced soy sauce

1 teaspoon sesame oil

1$^1/_2$ teaspoons cornflour (cornstarch)

Each serving provides
1832 kJ, 438 kcal, 32 g protein, 29 g fat (4 g saturated fat), 13 g carbohydrate (11 g sugars), 3 g fibre, 541 mg sodium

Chicken satay salad

This delicious salad is prepared with marinated strips of chicken that have first been threaded onto skewers and grilled. The chicken is served on a bed of rice and crunchy vegetables and drizzled with a spicy peanut dressing. It makes a great light meal for any occasion.

PREPARATION 20 minutes, plus at least 3 hours marinating   COOKING 25 minutes   SERVES 4

550 g (1¼ lb) skinless, boneless chicken breast fillets

2 tablespoons sunflower oil

3 tablespoons salt-reduced soy sauce

1 tablespoon fish sauce

2 cloves garlic, crushed

1 tablespoon grated fresh ginger

2¼ cups (250 g) basmati rice, rinsed

1 cup (100 g) sliced snow peas (mangetout)

finely grated zest of 2 limes

freshly squeezed juice of 2 limes

2 tablespoons chopped fresh coriander (cilantro) leaves

3 cups (225 g) shredded Chinese cabbage (wombok)

¼ telegraph (long) cucumber, diced

4 spring onions (scallions), sliced

SPICY PEANUT DRESSING

1 small onion, finely chopped

3 tablespoons salt-reduced crunchy peanut butter

1 long red chilli, seeded and finely chopped

100 ml (3½ fl oz) low-fat coconut milk

1 teaspoon caster (superfine) sugar

Each serving provides
2898 kJ, 692 kcal, 43 g protein, 30 g fat
(8 g saturated fat), 62 g carbohydrate
(7 g sugars), 4 g fibre, 1227 mg sodium

1 Cut the chicken breasts into long strips about 1 cm (½ inch) thick. In a bowl, mix together 1 tablespoon of the sunflower oil, 2 tablespoons of the soy sauce, the fish sauce, garlic and ginger. Add the chicken and toss to coat. Cover with plastic wrap and refrigerate for at least 3 hours.

2 Cook the rice in a saucepan of boiling water for 10 minutes, or until almost tender. Add the snow peas and cook for a further 2 minutes. Refresh immediately in cold water and drain well. Set aside.

3 Combine the lime zest and juice with the remaining oil and soy sauce in a large bowl. Add the rice, snow peas, coriander, cabbage, cucumber and spring onions, and toss together until well combined. Arrange on a serving platter.

4 Preheat the grill (broiler) to high. Lift the strips of chicken out of the marinade, reserving the marinade, and thread onto metal skewers. Grill for 8-10 minutes, or until cooked through, turning once so the chicken cooks evenly.

5 To make the spicy peanut dressing, put the onion, peanut butter, chilli, coconut milk, sugar and reserved marinade into a small saucepan. Bring to the boil, then reduce the heat and simmer for about 5 minutes, stirring regularly – add 2-3 tablespoons water if the dressing is too thick.

6 Remove the chicken from the skewers and arrange over the salad. Drizzle the dressing over the top and serve the salad warm or at room temperature.

ANOTHER IDEA

If you want to serve this salad cold, slide the grilled chicken off the skewers and toss with the spicy peanut dressing to coat. Leave to cool, then refrigerate for 2-3 hours. When ready to serve, just add to the chilled rice salad.

Turkey and garlic stir-fry

PREPARATION 10 minutes   COOKING 10 minutes   SERVES 4

3 teaspoons vegetable oil

1 red capsicum (bell pepper), seeded
    and sliced

1 yellow capsicum (bell pepper), halved,
    seeded and sliced

3 cloves garlic, crushed

2 tablespoons fresh lime juice

1 tablespoon bottled teriyaki marinade

1 tablespoon grated fresh ginger

500 g (1 lb) skinless, boneless turkey
    breast fillets, thinly sliced

300 g (10 oz) spinach leaves, chopped

Each serving provides
923 kJ, 220 kcal, 30 g protein, 9 g fat
(2 g saturated fat), 7 g carbohydrate
(5 g sugars), 3 g fibre, 120 mg sodium

1   Heat the vegetable oil in a wok or large non-stick frying pan
    over medium heat. Add the capsicum, garlic, lime juice,
    teriyaki marinade and ginger and stir-fry for 3 minutes,
    or until the capsicum is tender.

2   Add the turkey to the pan and stir-fry for 3–4 minutes, then
    add the spinach and stir-fry for 1 minute, or until the spinach
    has wilted and the turkey is cooked. Serve immediately with
    steamed rice.

HEALTHY EATING

Skinless turkey breast has about the same amount of protein as
lean beef, but contains less saturated fat than any other meat.

Chinese-style omelette

PREPARATION 20 minutes   COOKING 10 minutes   SERVES 4

1   Preheat the grill (broiler) to high. Use your hands to mix together the minced turkey with 1 teaspoon of the soy sauce until well combined. Heat the sunflower oil in a heavy-based ovenproof frying pan, add the turkey and cook for 3-5 minutes, breaking up any large lumps with a spoon, until lightly browned. Add the cabbage, bean sprouts, peas, smoked turkey, water chestnuts, spring onion and coriander and stir-fry for about 2-3 minutes, or until the vegetables have softened slightly.

2   Lightly beat the eggs with the garlic, ginger, sherry and remaining soy sauce. Add to the pan, pouring the egg mixture evenly over the vegetables and turkey. Cook, stirring gently with a wooden spatula and lifting the sides of the omelette to let the uncooked egg mixture run onto the pan, until the omelette is set. Slide the pan under the grill and cook briefly to set the egg on top.

3   Meanwhile, mix together the sesame oil, bean sauce, balsamic vinegar and chilli sauce in a bowl.

4   Cut the omelette into wedges and serve drizzled with the sauce mixture and garnished with extra coriander.

100 g (3^1/$_2$ oz) minced (ground) turkey

2 teaspoons soy sauce

2 tablespoons sunflower oil

2^2/$_3$ cups (200 g) shredded Chinese cabbage (wombok)

1 cup (90 g) bean sprouts, trimmed

^{1}/$_4$ cup (35 g) frozen peas

125 g (4 oz) slices smoked turkey or chicken, chopped

^{2}/$_3$ cup (110 g) canned water chestnuts, sliced

2 spring onions (scallions), thinly sliced

2 tablespoons fresh coriander (cilantro) leaves, chopped, plus extra, to serve

6 eggs

2 cloves garlic, finely chopped

2 teaspoons grated fresh ginger

2 tablespoons dry sherry

^{1}/$_2$ teaspoon sesame oil

1^1/$_2$ tablespoons black bean sauce

1 tablespoon balsamic vinegar

chilli sauce, to taste

Each serving provides
1501 kJ, 358 kcal, 31 g protein, 21 g fat (4 g saturated fat), 10 g carbohydrate (6 g sugars), 3 g fibre, 710 mg sodium

Citrus duck stir-fry

Zesty orange and warm Chinese spices perfectly complement the rich taste of duck in this stir-fry, which is cooked to tasty perfection with fresh green vegetables and healthy bean sprouts. Duck is an impressive dish to serve when entertaining.

PREPARATION 30 minutes, plus at least 2-3 hours marinating   COOKING 10 minutes   SERVES 4

1 Mix together the Chinese five-spice, soy sauce, sesame oil and $^{1}/_{2}$ tablespoon of the orange juice in a bowl and add to the duck, tossing to coat. Cover with plastic wrap and refrigerate for at least 2-3 hours. Return the duck to room temperature before cooking.

2 Meanwhile, peel the zest from half of one of the oranges, then cut it into fine strips. Add the strips to a saucepan of cold water, bring to the boil, then drain through a strainer and set the strips aside. Cut away all the peel and white pith from the oranges using a sharp knife, then cut the flesh into segments and set aside.

3 Heat the sugar and vinegar in a small saucepan until the sugar has dissolved. Blend the cornflour with 1 tablespoon of the orange juice, then pour the remaining orange juice into the saucepan. Bring to the boil, then add the cornflour mixture, stirring constantly until the sauce has thickened. Add the orange zest strips, then turn off the heat.

4 Remove the duck from the marinade with a slotted spoon. Heat 1 tablespoon of the vegetable oil in a wok or large non-stick frying pan over medium-high heat. Add the duck and stir-fry for 2-3 minutes, or until tender. Remove to a plate and set aside.

5 Add the remaining oil to the wok, add the spring onions and snow peas and stir-fry for 1 minute. Add the bean sprouts and stir-fry for 2 minutes, or until tender but crisp.

6 Return the duck to the pan with the orange segments, orange sauce and any remaining marinade. Bring to the boil and let it cook for about 30 seconds, or until everything is heated through. Serve immediately.

$^{1}/_{4}$ teaspoon Chinese five-spice
1 tablespoon soy sauce
2 teaspoons sesame oil
100 ml ($3^{1}/_{2}$ fl oz) fresh orange juice
2 x 175 g (6 oz) skinless, boneless duck breasts, thinly sliced
2 oranges
1 tablespoon caster (superfine) sugar
1 tablespoon red wine vinegar
1 teaspoon cornflour (cornstarch)
$1^{1}/_{2}$ tablespoons vegetable oil
4 spring onions (scallions), sliced
125 g (4 oz) snow peas (mangetout), halved lengthwise
$2^{1}/_{4}$ cups (200 g) bean sprouts, trimmed

Each serving provides
1018 kJ, 244 kcal, 19 g protein, 15 g fat (3 g saturated fat), 10 g carbohydrate (8 g sugars), 3 g fibre, 336 mg sodium

Asian-style duck pancakes

These freshly pan-fried pancakes taste exquisite served with a simple filling of roast Peking duck, crisp fresh cucumber and spring onions (scallions). It is easy to prepare most of the meal in advance, making it a perfect dinner idea for easy entertaining.

PREPARATION 25 minutes   COOKING 15 minutes   SERVES 8

PANCAKES

1/2 cup (75 g) plain (all-purpose) flour
2 tablespoons cornflour (cornstarch)
1/4 cup (60 ml) low-fat milk
2 eggs, lightly beaten
1 tablespoon butter, melted, or canola oil
rice bran or canola oil spray

FILLING

500 g (1 lb) roast Peking duck, meat thinly sliced, skin and bones discarded
3 spring onions (scallions)
1/2 Lebanese (short) cucumber, seeded and cut into matchsticks
1/4 cup (60 ml) hoisin sauce

Each serving provides
944 kJ, 226 kcal, 18 g protein, 11 g fat
(4 g saturated fat), 13 g carbohydrate
(4 g sugars), 1 g fibre, 207 mg sodium

1   To make the pancakes, put the flour, cornflour, milk, eggs, melted butter and 1/4 cup (60 ml) water in a bowl and whisk until well combined and smooth. Pour into a jug, cover with plastic wrap, and set aside for 15 minutes.

2   Heat a wok or large non-stick frying pan over medium heat, lightly spray with oil and, when hot, pour 1 1/2 tablespoons of batter into the wok. Working quickly, tilt the wok to spread the mixture out to form a thin pancake with a 15 cm (6 inch) diameter. Cook for 2 minutes, then turn and cook the other side for a further 1 minute, flattening any air bubbles that may appear. Remove to a plate and keep warm. Repeat with remaining mixture to make 8 pancakes in total.

3   To serve, place some of the duck meat in the centre of each pancake, top with some spring onions and cucumber and drizzle over 1 teaspoon hoisin sauce. Roll up and serve immediately. Alternatively, arrange all of the ingredients on a platter so guests can make their own.

ANOTHER IDEA

If you are in a hurry you can make the pancakes in advance and refrigerate until required, or freeze them with a sheet of baking (parchment) paper between each pancake for easy removal. You will need to defrost and reheat in a frying pan before serving.

Braised duck with crunchy salad

Braising boneless duck breasts in red wine with garlic and ginger, plus
a little redcurrant jelly for sweetness, produces moist and tender meat.
The duck is cut into strips and served on a colourful mixture of crisp raw
vegetables, oranges and water chestnuts.

PREPARATION 20 minutes   COOKING 30 minutes   SERVES 4

1 Preheat the oven to 220°C (425°F/Gas 7). Remove all of
   the skin and fat from the duck breasts. Place them in an
   ovenproof dish, pour over the wine and add the redcurrant
   jelly, garlic and ginger. Cook the duck for 20-25 minutes,
   or until tender.

2 Meanwhile, mix together the extra virgin olive oil and
   vinegar in a large salad bowl. Cut the peel and pith from the
   oranges with a sharp knife and, holding each orange over
   the bowl to catch the juice, cut between the membrane to
   release the segments. Add them to the bowl. Add the red
   cabbage, Chinese cabbage, bean sprouts, watercress
   (reserving a few sprigs to use for garnish) and water
   chestnuts. Toss well to coat everything with the dressing.

3 Remove the duck from the oven and keep warm. Pour the
   cooking liquid into a saucepan. Boil the liquid rapidly for
   1-2 minutes to reduce slightly. To serve, cut the duck
   diagonally across the grain into neat slices. Pour the wine
   sauce over the salad and toss to combine. Pile the slices of
   duck on top, garnish with the reserved sprigs of watercress
   and serve immediately.

ANOTHER IDEA
You can substitute a variety of other vegetables in this salad. Try
adding lightly cooked baby corn, sliced raw zucchini (courgette)
or steamed asparagus spears. You can also sprinkle over some
toasted cashew nuts for extra crunch.

500 g (1 lb) boneless duck breasts
$1/2$ cup (125 ml) red wine
1 tablespoon redcurrant jelly
1 clove garlic, crushed
1 teaspoon grated fresh ginger
2 tablespoons extra virgin olive oil
2 teaspoons balsamic or sherry vinegar
2 oranges
3 cups (225 g) shredded red cabbage
$1/4$ Chinese cabbage (wombok),
   shredded
$1 2/3$ cups (150 g) bean sprouts
$2 3/4$ cups (85 g) watercress
$1 1/3$ cups (210 g) drained canned water
   chestnuts, sliced

Each serving provides
1475 kJ, 352 kcal, 27 g protein, 17 g fat
(4 g saturated fat), 18 g carbohydrate
(15 g sugars), 7 g fibre, 34 mg sodium

Beef, lamb & pork

Beef pho

This Vietnamese noodle soup with beef is traditionally served with accompaniments such as fresh herbs, chilli or lime, which guests add to the hot steaming soup as they like. This soup is so satisfying it can easily be served as main course.

PREPARATION 15 minutes   COOKING 20 minutes   SERVES 4

4 cups (1 litre) salt-reduced beef stock

1 teaspoon grated fresh ginger

1 cinnamon stick

2 star anise

2 green cardamom pods, bruised

1/2 teaspoon coriander seeds, toasted

1 tablespoon fish sauce

250 g (8 oz) rice vermicelli

200 g (7 oz) sirloin steak, trimmed and
    thinly sliced

4 cups (120 g) fresh coriander (cilantro)
    leaves (optional)

2 1/2 cups (50 g) fresh Vietnamese mint
    (optional)

1 cup (90 g) bean sprouts, trimmed
    (optional)

1 long red chilli, seeded and sliced
    (optional)

1 lime, cut into wedges (optional)

1/3 cup (80 ml) hoisin sauce (optional)

Each serving provides
1487 kJ, 355 kcal, 19 g protein, 4 g fat
(1 g saturated fat), 57 g carbohydrate
(2 g sugars), 1 g fibre, 1597 mg sodium

1 Place the stock, ginger, cinnamon stick, star anise, cardamom pods, coriander seeds and fish sauce in a large saucepan or stockpot with 4 cups (1 litre) water and bring to the boil. Reduce the heat to low and simmer for 10–15 minutes, or until aromatic.

2 Meanwhile, soak the noodles according to the packet instructions. Drain well and set aside.

3 Strain the stock, then return to the pan and bring back to the boil, discarding the spices. Add the steak and simmer for about 5 minutes, or until the meat is cooked. Divide the noodles among serving bowls, pile the steak on top and ladle over the hot stock.

4 Serve the beef pho with the coriander, mint, bean sprouts, chilli, lime wedges and hoisin sauce passed separately so that guests can help themselves.

HEALTHY EATING

Beef is a great source of protein but choose lean cuts of steak and make sure they are trimmed of fat before slicing.

Thai beef with papaya and rice

PREPARATION 20 minutes, plus 20 minutes marinating   COOKING 15 minutes   SERVES 4

1 To make the Thai lime dressing, mix all of the ingredients together in a small bowl. Spoon 1/4 cup (60 ml) of the dressing over the steak, turning to coat, and refrigerate for at least 20 minutes. Reserve the remaining dressing.

2 Put the rice in a saucepan with the stock, kaffir lime leaves and 600 ml (21 fl oz) water. Bring to the boil, then reduce the heat to low, cover and simmer for 10 minutes. Drain well and set aside.

3 Meanwhile, pat the steak dry with paper towels. Heat the vegetable oil in a wok or large non-stick frying pan over high heat. Cook the steak for 2–3 minutes on each side for rare, or until cooked to your liking. Remove the steak from the pan and leave to rest for 5 minutes.

4 Put the papaya, cucumber, mint, coriander and red onion in a bowl. Add all but 1 1/2 tablespoons of the remaining dressing and toss gently to combine.

5 Divide the rice among serving plates, arrange the lettuce leaves alongside topped with the papaya salad. Slice the steak into thin strips and arrange over the salad. Drizzle the remaining dressing over the top and sprinkle with the peanuts, then serve at room temperature.

ANOTHER IDEA

Kaffir lime (makrut) leaves are a citrus fruit from South-East Asia. Although not a true lime they are popular in regional cooking and add a delicate flavour to this dish. If they are unavailable, substitute with the finely grated zest of 1 lime.

400 g (14 oz) lean sirloin steak

1 1/4 cups (250 g) jasmine rice (Thai fragrant rice)

600 ml (21 fl oz) salt-reduced chicken stock

4 kaffir lime (makrut) leaves, crushed

2 teaspoons vegetable oil

2 firm, ripe papayas (pawpaw), peeled, seeded and sliced

1/2 small telegraph (long) cucumber, halved lengthwise, seeded and sliced

20 fresh mint leaves, shredded

1/4 cup (7 g) fresh coriander (cilantro) leaves, chopped

1 red onion, thinly sliced

1 cos (romaine) lettuce, leaves separated

unsalted peanuts, roasted and chopped, to serve

THAI LIME DRESSING

1 1/2 tablespoons vegetable oil

1 1/2 tablespoons fish sauce

1 1/2 tablespoons salt-reduced soy sauce

1 tablespoon honey

finely grated zest of 1 lime

juice of 1 lime

1 long red chilli, seeded and chopped

2 cloves garlic, crushed

Each serving provides
2306 kJ, 551 kcal, 30 g protein, 16 g fat
(4 g saturated fat), 72 g carbohydrate
(16 g sugars), 4 g fibre, 1415 mg sodium

Beef, lamb & pork

Thai beef and broccoli salad

This wonderful Thai salad with fresh mint, basil, coriander (cilantro) and lime makes a perfect light lunch or dinner idea. The tender lean steak works perfectly with the crisp crunch of lightly steamed broccoli and is terrifically good for you as well.

PREPARATION 5 minutes, plus 10 minutes marinating   COOKING 10 minutes   SERVES 4

500 g (1 lb) lean rump (round) steak
1/2 cup (125 ml) salt-reduced soy sauce
2 cloves garlic, crushed
1/3 cup (80 ml) fresh lime juice
1 cup (60 g) small broccoli florets
1/3 cup (5 g) fresh mint
1/3 cup (5 g) fresh basil
1/4 cup (7 g) fresh coriander (cilantro) leaves
1/2 telegraph (long) cucumber, sliced
2 long red chillies, seeded and sliced
2 teaspoons soft brown sugar

Each serving provides
829 kJ, 198 kcal, 30 g protein, 6 g fat
(3 g saturated fat), 6 g carbohydrate
(3 g sugars), 2 g fibre, 1216 mg sodium

1   Put the steak in large bowl with 1/4 cup (60 ml) of the soy sauce, the garlic and 2 tablespoons of the lime juice. Turn to coat the steak and set aside for 10 minutes.

2   Heat a chargrill pan or large non-stick frying pan over high heat. Cook the steak for 1-2 minutes on each side for rare, or until cooked to your liking. Set aside to cool.

3   Steam the broccoli in a steamer set over a saucepan of boiling water for 5-6 minutes, or until just tender. Refresh immediately under cold water, drain, and allow to cool. Place in a large bowl with the mint, basil, coriander and cucumber.

4   Thinly slice the steak and add to the broccoli in the bowl. Combine the chilli, sugar, remaining soy sauce and lime juice and pour over the steak and broccoli, tossing gently to combine. Divide among serving plates and serve.

HEALTHY EATING
When it is overcooked broccoli loses both flavour and nutritional value, so steaming it is the best method to retain its wonderful health benefits. Among other things, broccoli contains high levels of vitamins A, C and K as well as fibre and folate.

Asparagus, broccoli and beef stir-fry

PREPARATION 15 minutes, plus 15 minutes marinating   COOKING 10 minutes   SERVES 4

500 g (1 lb) lean rump (round) steak, thinly sliced across the grain

2¹/₂ tablespoons oyster sauce

3 teaspoons salt-reduced soy sauce

¹/₂ teaspoon sugar

2 tablespoons cornflour (cornstarch)

2 cloves garlic, chopped

2 tablespoons vegetable oil

1 small onion, cut into wedges

1 small carrot, peeled and sliced

1 red capsicum (bell pepper), halved, seeded and sliced

1 cup (90 g) small broccoli florets

5 fresh or canned baby corn, halved lengthwise

1 bunch asparagus, trimmed and cut diagonally into 5 cm (2 inch) lengths

Each serving provides
1200 kJ, 287 kcal, 27 protein, 15 g fat
(4 g saturated fat), 11 g carbohydrate
(5 g sugars), 3 g fibre, 792 mg sodium

1   Put the steak in a bowl with the oyster and soy sauces, sugar, cornflour and garlic. Mix together and set aside for at least 15 minutes to marinate.

2   Heat 1 tablespoon of the vegetable oil in a wok or large, non-stick frying pan over high heat. Add the steak and stir-fry for about 3 minutes, or until it is cooked to your liking. Remove from the pan, set aside and keep warm.

3   Heat the remaining oil in the clean wok over medium heat. Add the onion, carrot, capsicum and broccoli and stir-fry for 1 minute. Add the corn, asparagus and ¹/₂ cup (125 ml) water and then return the steak to the wok and cook for a further 1 minute, or until the sauce has thickened – the vegetables should be slightly softened but still retain their crispness. Divide among serving plates and serve immediately.

HEALTHY EATING

An excellent source of dietary fibre and folate, asparagus also contains a range of vitamins and minerals, including some B-group vitamins, vitamins C and K, manganese, copper, phosphorus and potassium.

Chinese beef and leek with noodles

PREPARATION 20 minutes   COOKING 5 minutes   SERVES 2

1   Put the steak in a bowl with the cornflour and Chinese five-spice. Toss to coat the steak.

2   Put the carrot, leek, spring onion and capsicum in a large bowl and toss to combine. Combine the soy sauce, rice wine and 1½ tablespoons of water in a small bowl.

3   Soak the noodles according to the packet instructions. Drain well and set aside.

4   Heat 1 tablespoon of the vegetable oil in a wok or large non-stick frying pan over high heat. Add the steak and stir-fry for 2–3 minutes, or until cooked through. Remove to a plate. Add the remaining oil, then add the garlic, ginger and chilli and stir-fry for 30 seconds. Add the combined carrot, leek, spring onions and capsicum and stir-fry for a further 1 minute, or until just tender.

5   Add the soy sauce mixture to the wok, and as soon as the sauce is bubbling, add the noodles and steak and toss to combine and heat through. Divide between serving bowls and serve immediately, with a few drops of soy sauce over the top, to taste.

200 g (7 oz) lean rump (round) steak, thinly sliced across the grain

2 teaspoons cornflour (cornstarch)

1 teaspoon Chinese five-spice

1 carrot, cut into matchsticks

1 small leek, white part only, cut into matchsticks

6 spring onions (scallions), sliced diagonally

½ red capsicum (bell pepper), seeded and sliced

1½ tablespoons salt-reduced soy sauce, plus extra, to serve

1½ tablespoons shaoxing rice wine

100 g (3½ oz) rice vermicelli

1½ tablespoons vegetable oil

1 clove garlic, finely chopped

2 teaspoons grated fresh ginger

1 long red chilli, seeded and finely chopped

Each serving provides
2128 kJ, 508 kcal, 26 g protein. 19 g fat (4 g saturated fat), 53 g carbohydrate (7 g sugars), 5 g fibre, 727 mg sodium

Beef and black bean stir-fry

Beef in black bean sauce is one of the classic dishes that everyone knows from their local Chinese restaurant. Try this homemade version — you'll be able to control the amount of fat used so you know you're getting a healthy and delicious meal.

PREPARATION 10 minutes   COOKING 10 minutes   SERVES 4

1   Combine the steak, oil and ginger in a small bowl, turning to coat. Heat a wok or large non-stick frying pan over high heat. Add the steak in small batches and stir-fry for 1–2 minutes. Remove to a plate and repeat until all the steak is cooked through.

2   Add the capsicum, celery and snow peas to the wok with a sprinkling of water. Steam for 2–3 minutes, then return the steak to the wok. Stir in the black bean sauce and heat through, stirring constantly, for about 1–2 minutes. Divide among serving bowls and top with the almonds.

ANOTHER IDEA
You can replace the snow peas with any fresh green vegetables — for a variation of flavour and texture, why not try trimmed green beans or sugar snap peas, small broccoli florets or even Chinese broccoli (gai larn) instead.

500 g (1 lb) lean sirloin steak, trimmed and cut into thin strips
2 teaspoons vegetable oil
1 teaspoon grated fresh ginger
1 red capsicum (bell pepper), halved, seeded and sliced
2 celery stalks, sliced
200 g (7 oz) snow peas (mangetout), trimmed
1/4 cup (60 ml) black bean sauce
2 tablespoons slivered almonds

Each serving provides
1106 kJ, 264 kcal, 30 g protein, 12 g fat (3 g saturated fat), 8 g carbohydrate (6 g sugars), 3 g fibre, 787 mg sodium

Tender beef with fried rice

Stir-fries are a simple way to incorporate a variety of meat, vegetables and grains into your diet in one dish. Here, thin slices of steak team with fried rice and colourful vegetables to make a delicious combination of textures and flavours.

PREPARATION 15 minutes   COOKING 20 minutes   SERVES 4

2 tablespoons sunflower oil

300 g (10 oz) lean rump (round) steak, trimmed and thinly sliced

1 clove garlic, thinly sliced

1 tablespoon grated fresh ginger

2 red onions, cut into wedges

1 large red capsicum (bell pepper), halved, seeded and sliced

3 cups (180 g) small broccoli florets

2 tablespoons oyster sauce

2 tablespoons fresh coriander (cilantro) leaves

FRIED RICE

1 cup (200 g) long-grain white rice

1 tablespoon sunflower oil

4 spring onions (scallions), sliced

2/3 cup (100 g) frozen peas

2 eggs, lightly beaten

1 tablespoon salt-reduced soy sauce

Each serving provides
2032 kJ, 485 kcal, 28 g protein, 20 g fat (4 g saturated fat), 46 g carbohydrate (7 g sugars), 4 g fibre, 735 mg sodium

1   To make the fried rice, cook the rice in a saucepan of boiling water for 10-12 minutes, or until tender. Drain well and cool. Heat the sunflower oil in a wok or large non-stick frying pan over medium-high heat. Add the spring onions and peas and stir-fry for 1 minute, then pour in the eggs and soy sauce and continue stirring until the eggs begin to set. Add the rice and stir well to combine, then cook for a further 1 minute without stirring. Remove from the heat, set aside and keep warm.

2   Heat 1 tablespoon of the sunflower oil in a wok or large non-stick frying pan and swirl to coat the base and side. Add the steak, garlic and ginger and stir-fry for 2 minutes, or until the steak is browned all over. Remove from the wok and set aside.

3   Heat the remaining oil in the wok until hot, then add the onions, capsicum and broccoli florets. Stir-fry for 2 minutes or until the onion begins to colour. Return the steak mixture and any juices to the wok, then add the oyster sauce and 2 tablespoons water and simmer for 1 minute.

4   Divide the fried rice among serving bowls and top with the steak and vegetables. Garnish with the coriander leaves and serve immediately.

ANOTHER IDEA

You can replace the steak in this dish with thinly sliced boneless lean pork loin steak or chops if you wish. You can also add a seeded and thinly sliced long red chilli to the vegetables when stir-frying for added kick, and serve with noodles instead of rice.

Hoisin beef stir-fry

PREPARATION 15 minutes   COOKING 5 minutes   SERVES 2

175 g (6 oz) wok-ready hokkien (egg)
    noodles

1 tablespoon sunflower oil

2 large cloves garlic, crushed

1 teaspoon grated fresh ginger

1 large red capsicum (bell pepper), seeded
    and thinly sliced

125 g (4 oz) small button mushrooms,
    halved

200 g (7 oz) lean sirloin steak, thinly
    sliced across the grain

85 g (3 oz) snow peas (mangetout),
    halved lengthwise

4 spring onions (scallions), sliced

1/4 cup (60 ml) hoisin sauce

1 tablespoon salt-reduced soy sauce

1 teaspoon sesame oil (optional)

Each serving provides
2428 kJ, 580 kcal, 35 g protein, 21 g fat
(5 g saturated fat), 63 g carbohydrate
(16 g sugars), 9 g fibre, 939 mg sodium

1   Soak the noodles according to the packet instructions,
    then drain well and set aside.

2   Heat the sunflower oil in a wok or large non-stick frying pan
    over high heat. Add the garlic and ginger and stir-fry for
    1 minute, then add the capsicum and mushrooms and stir-fry
    for about 2-3 minutes, or until the capsicum starts to soften.

3   Add the steak, snow peas and spring onions to the wok and
    stir-fry for a further 1-2 minutes, or until it is cooked to
    your liking.

4   Add the hoisin and soy sauces to the wok and stir well until
    bubbling, then drizzle in the sesame oil, if using. Divide
    the noodles between serving bowls and serve with the steak
    and vegetables over the top.

ANOTHER IDEA

You can omit the noodles in this recipe if you like and simply
cook the steak and vegetables together following the method
above. Serve with steamed rice on the side instead.

Teriyaki beef with mushrooms

PREPARATION 15 minutes, plus at least 15 minutes marinating   COOKING 15 minutes   SERVES 4

1. Put the steak in a bowl with the teriyaki marinade and refrigerate for at least 15 minutes, or up to 3 hours.

2. In a separate bowl, combine the hoisin sauce, cornflour and $^1/_3$ cup (80 ml) of the stock. Set aside.

3. Heat 1 teaspoon of the vegetable oil in a wok or large non-stick frying pan over high heat. Add the spring onions and stir-fry for 1 minute. Remove to a large bowl.

4. Add the steak and garlic to the wok and stir-fry for about 2 minutes, or until the steak is cooked to your liking. Transfer to the bowl. Heat another 1 teaspoon of the oil, then add the mushrooms to the wok and stir-fry for about 3 minutes, or until they begin to soften, then transfer to the bowl. Heat the remaining oil, add the sugar snap peas and capsicum and stir-fry for 1–2 minutes, or until they soften.

5. Return the steak and all of the vegetables to the wok and stir in the remaining stock. Cover and cook over medium heat for 2–3 minutes, or until the ingredients are heated through and the vegetables are just tender. Whisk the hoisin sauce mixture, add to the wok and continue to stir-fry until the sauce boils, then cook for a further 1 minute. Divide among serving bowls and serve immediately.

350 g (12 oz) lean sirloin steak, thinly sliced across the grain
2 tablespoons bottled teriyaki marinade
2 tablespoons hoisin sauce
2 tablespoons cornflour (cornstarch)
$1^1/_4$ cups (310 ml) salt-reduced chicken stock
3 teaspoons vegetable oil
4 spring onions (scallions), thinly sliced
2 cloves garlic, crushed
1 cup (90 g) sliced shiitake mushrooms
250 g (8 oz) sugar snap peas or snow peas (mangetout), trimmed
2 large red capsicums (bell peppers), halved, seeded and sliced

Each serving provides
1045 kJ, 250 kcal, 22 g protein, 9 g fat
(3 g saturated fat), 18 g carbohydrate
(11 g sugars), 3 g fibre, 453 mg sodium

Stir-fried beef and vegetables

For a quick and easy meal idea it is hard to beat this simple Asian stir-fry that is both colourful and a pleasure to eat. You can serve the beef and vegetables with steamed rice on the side or over your favourite cooked noodles for a heartier dinner.

PREPARATION 15 minutes, plus 20 minutes marinating   COOKING 15 minutes   SERVES 4

1   Mix 1 tablespoon of the soy sauce with all of the sugar in a bowl. Add the steak, tossing to coat, and set aside to marinate for at least 20 minutes. Steam the broccoli in a steamer set over a saucepan of boiling water for 5-6 minutes, or until just tender. Refresh immediately under cold water, drain, and allow to cool.

2   Heat the vegetable oil in a wok or large non-stick frying pan over high heat. Add the steak and stir-fry for 5 minutes, or until cooked to your liking. Remove to a plate.

3   Add the mushrooms, capsicum, snow peas, spring onions, garlic, ginger and chilli flakes to the wok and stir-fry for 3-4 minutes, or until the snow peas are just tender.

4   Combine the stock, remaining soy sauce, vinegar and cornflour in a small bowl until smooth. Add to wok, bring to the boil and cook until the sauce thickens. Add the broccoli and cook for 2 minutes, or until heated through.

5   Drain the steak, add to the wok and cook for a further 30 seconds to heat through. Divide among serving bowls and serve immediately.

HEALTHY EATING

Stir-frying keeps all the water-soluble vitamins and minerals from the vegetables in the dish rather than pouring them down the sink with the cooking water. It's also a very quick method of cooking, so there is minimal nutrient loss.

1/4 cup (60 ml) salt-reduced soy sauce

2 teaspoons dark brown sugar

500 g (1 lb) lean rump (round) steak, sliced thinly across the grain

3 cups (180 g) small broccoli florets

2 tablespoons vegetable oil

2 cups (180 g) sliced shiitake mushrooms

1 red capsicum (bell pepper), seeded and thinly sliced

150 g (5 oz) snow peas (mangetout), trimmed

4 spring onions (scallions), thinly sliced

2 cloves garlic, crushed

1 tablespoon grated fresh ginger

1 pinch of dried red chilli flakes

1/3 cup (80 ml) salt-reduced chicken stock

1 tablespoon balsamic vinegar

2 teaspoons cornflour (cornstarch)

Each serving provides
1318 kJ, 315 kcal, 32 g protein, 15 g fat
(4 g saturated fat), 11 g carbohydrate
(8 g sugars), 4 g fibre, 699 mg sodium

Sizzling stir-fried kidneys

This is a deliciously different way to serve kidneys – tossed with Chinese egg noodles and a medley of tender Asian vegetables in a garlic and black bean sauce. If you love strong flavours, it's the perfect recipe for you.

PREPARATION 15 minutes   COOKING 20 minutes   SERVES 2

125 g (4 oz) wok-ready hokkien (egg) noodles

175 g (6 oz) calf's kidneys

2 tablespoons black bean sauce

1 tablespoon sunflower oil

1 small red onion, halved and thinly sliced

1 yellow capsicum (bell pepper), halved, seeded and sliced

1 red birdseye (Thai) chilli, seeded and finely chopped

1 tablespoon grated fresh ginger

2 cloves garlic, finely chopped

2³/4 cups (250 g) bean sprouts, trimmed

300 g (10 oz) bok choy, chopped

1¹/2 cups (50 g) rocket (arugula) leaves

2 tablespoons salt-reduced soy sauce, or to taste

2 tablespoons toasted sesame seeds

Each serving provides
2112 kJ, 505 kcal, 33 g protein, 20 g fat (3 g saturated fat), 48 g carbohydrate (10 g sugars), 10 g fibre, 1787 mg sodium

1 Cook the noodles according to the packet instructions. Drain well and set aside.

2 Cut the kidneys into 2.5 cm (1 inch) pieces, following the lobes and discarding any fat and membranes. Dilute the black bean sauce with 2 tablespoons water and set aside.

3 Heat 1 teaspoon of the sunflower oil in a wok or large non-stick frying pan over medium-high heat. Add the kidneys and stir-fry for 3 minutes, or until they are evenly browned, then add 1 tablespoon of the black bean sauce mixture and stir well. Remove to a plate and keep warm.

4 Heat the remaining oil in the clean wok and swirl to coat the base and side. Add the onion, capsicum, chilli, ginger and garlic and stir-fry for 1 minute. Add the noodles, bean sprouts, bok choy and rocket. Sprinkle over 2 tablespoons water and continue stir-frying for 2 minutes – the vegetables should still be crunchy and the greens wilted.

5 Add the remaining black bean sauce mixture, the soy sauce and the kidneys to the wok and toss well to combine. Divide between serving bowls and serve immediately, sprinkled with the sesame seeds.

HEALTHY EATING

Kidneys are a valuable source of iron and protein and also provide selenium, a mineral that acts as an antioxidant, protecting cells against damage by free radicals. Selenium also plays a major role in the maintenance of healthy skin and hair.

Thai-style beef sandwiches

PREPARATION 20 minutes, plus at least 30 minutes marinating   COOKING 10 minutes   SERVES 4

2 tablespoons tomato paste
　　(concentrated purée)

1½ teaspoons ground coriander

½ cup (125 ml) fresh lime juice

500 g (1 lb) lean sirloin steak

1 teaspoon sugar

½ teaspoon salt

1 teaspoon dried red chilli flakes

3 cups (225 g) shredded green cabbage

2 carrots, coarsely grated

1 large red capsicum (bell pepper),
　　halved, seeded and sliced

½ cup (15 g) chopped fresh coriander
　　(cilantro) leaves

⅓ cup (7 g) chopped fresh mint

4 bread rolls, halved

Each serving provides
1805 kJ, 431 kcal, 34 g protein, 11 g fat
(4 g saturated fat), 49 g carbohydrate
(10 g sugars), 7 g fibre, 888 mg sodium

1　Combine the tomato paste, ground coriander and ¼ cup
(60 ml) of the lime juice in a bowl. Add the steak, turning to
coat, and refrigerate for at least 30 minutes.

2　Whisk the remaining lime juice in a large bowl with the sugar,
salt and chilli flakes. Add the cabbage, carrots, capsicum,
coriander and mint and toss well to combine. Cover with
plastic wrap and refrigerate until needed.

3　Heat a chargrill pan or barbecue hotplate to high. Cook the
steak for 4 minutes on each side, brushing any remaining
marinade over the steak halfway through, until cooked to
your liking. Leave to rest for 10 minutes, then thinly slice
across the grain.

4　To serve, fill each bread roll with some of the cabbage
mixture and top with the steak. Serve immediately.

ANOTHER IDEA

Instead of serving with bread rolls, you can wrap the steak
and salad in pita bread for a lighter meal idea, or simply serve
alongside some steamed rice.

Beef, lamb & pork

Thai red beef curry

PREPARATION 10 minutes   COOKING 10 minutes   SERVES 4

1   Combine the steak, vegetable oil and garlic in a bowl, tossing to coat. Heat a wok or large non-stick frying pan over high heat. Add the steak and stir-fry for 1–2 minutes, or until cooked to your liking. Remove to a plate.

2   Add the capsicum and mushrooms to the clean wok with a sprinkling of water and steam for 1–2 minutes, or until softened slightly.

3   Return the steak to the wok, then stir in the curry paste, sugar, fish sauce, coconut milk, stock, spinach and coriander. Bring to the boil, then reduce the heat and simmer for 1–2 minutes, or until the spinach has wilted. Serve the curry over a bed of steamed rice, if desired.

500 g (1 lb) lean sirloin steak, thinly sliced across the grain

2 teaspoons vegetable oil

1 clove garlic, crushed

$^1/_2$ red capsicum (bell pepper), halved, seeded and thinly sliced

1 cup (90 g) sliced button mushrooms

1 tablespoon red curry paste (see page 248)

1 tablespoon soft brown sugar

1 tablespoon fish sauce

200 ml (7 fl oz) low-fat coconut milk

$^2/_3$ cup (150 ml) salt-reduced beef stock

2 cups (100 g) chopped spinach leaves

$^1/_3$ cup (10 g) fresh coriander (cilantro) leaves

Each serving provides
1215 kJ, 290 kcal, 30 g protein, 15 g fat (8 g saturated fat), 9 g carbohydrate (5 g sugars), 2 g fibre, 693 mg sodium

Japanese shabu shabu

Japanese-style fondue includes thin strips of lean beef, baby vegetables and udon noodles, all cooked at the table in simmering stock. Enjoy with Japanese dips and pickles for a fun, one-pot meal that is perfect for entertaining.

PREPARATION 30 minutes   COOKING (at table) 1 minute each forkful   SERVES 4

1   Wrap the steak in plastic wrap and chill in the freezer for about 20 minutes until firm but not solid (this makes it easier to slice).

2   Cook the noodles according to the packet instructions, then rinse immediately under cold water and drain well. Put into a serving bowl, add the sesame oil and toss gently to coat.

3   Heat the stock, soy sauce and ginger in a fondue pot. Set the pot over a fondue burner in the centre of the table. Arrange the steak, noodles, leeks, carrots, mushrooms and bok choy on a platter on the table. Put the wasabi, soy sauce, pickled ginger and pickled vegetables in separate, small side dishes.

4   To serve, let each person dip pieces of steak and vegetables into the simmering stock, using fondue forks, and swishing the food around briefly until lightly cooked. Eat with the wasabi (mix a tiny amount with soy sauce to make a 'hot' dip), ginger and pickles, to taste.

5   When all the steak and vegetables have been cooked, add the noodles to the stock, then divide among serving bowls. Season to taste with any remaining sauces and pickles and enjoy as a soup.

ANOTHER IDEA
You can replace any of the vegetables in this dish with your favourites. Use button mushrooms if shiitake are unavailable, or try florets of broccoli, cauliflower or turnips cut into thin strips.

400 g (14 oz) lean rump (round) or sirloin steak, thinly sliced across the grain

250 g (8 oz) udon (rice) noodles

2 teaspoons sesame oil

2 cups (500 ml) salt-reduced beef stock

1 teaspoon salt-reduced soy sauce, plus extra, to serve

1 teaspoon grated fresh ginger

100 g (3$\frac{1}{2}$ oz) baby leeks, white part only, trimmed and cut into short lengths

100 g (3$\frac{1}{2}$ oz) baby carrots, cut into matchsticks

100 g (3$\frac{1}{2}$ oz) shiitake mushrooms, halved

125 g (4 oz) baby bok choy, trimmed and quartered lengthwise

wasabi (Japanese horseradish), to serve

pickled ginger, to serve

pickled vegetables, to serve

Each serving provides
1262 kJ, 301 kcal, 27 g protein, 10 g fat (3 g saturated fat), 26 g carbohydrate (5 g sugars), 2 g fibre, 677 mg sodium

Sweet and sour pork

Sweet and sour sauce doesn't have to be thick, gluggy and bright orange. This modern, light version allows the succulence of the meat and the fresh flavours and different textures of a variety of vegetables and noodles to shine through.

PREPARATION 30 minutes   COOKING 20 minutes   SERVES 4

350 g (12 oz) pork fillet, trimmed and thinly sliced

1 tablespoon salt-reduced soy sauce

2 teaspoons cornflour (cornstarch)

150 g (5 oz) wok-ready hokkien (egg) noodles

2 tablespoons sunflower oil

8 fresh or canned baby corn, quartered lengthwise

1 large carrot, cut into matchsticks

1 large clove garlic, finely chopped

1 tablespoon grated fresh ginger

300 g (10 oz) bean sprouts, trimmed

4 spring onions (scallions), sliced

1 teaspoon sesame oil

SWEET AND SOUR SAUCE

1 tablespoon cornflour (cornstarch)

1 tablespoon soft brown sugar

1 tablespoon rice wine vinegar

2 tablespoons shaoxing rice wine or dry sherry

2 tablespoons tomato sauce (ketchup)

3 tablespoons salt-reduced soy sauce

425 g (15 oz) canned pineapple slices in natural juice, drained and chopped, with juice reserved

Each serving provides
1684 kJ, 402 kcal, 27 g protein, 13 g fat
(2 g saturated fat), 40 g carbohydrate
(16 g sugars), 6 g fibre, 903 mg sodium

1   Put the pork in a bowl with the soy sauce, season with black pepper and toss well to coat. Sprinkle over the cornflour and stir again. Cover with plastic wrap and set aside.

2   To make the sweet and sour sauce, combine the cornflour, sugar, vinegar, rice wine, tomato sauce, soy sauce and reserved pineapple juice in a small bowl. Set aside.

3   Cook the noodles according to the packet instructions, then drain well and set aside.

4   Heat 1 tablespoon of the sunflower oil in a wok or large non-stick frying pan and swirl to coat the base and side. Add the pork and stir-fry for 4-5 minutes, or until cooked to your liking. Remove to a plate.

5   Heat the remaining oil in the wok, then add the corn and stir-fry for 1 minute. Add the carrot, garlic and ginger and stir-fry for a further 1 minute. Sprinkle over $1/2$ cup (125 ml) water and let the vegetables steam for 2-3 minutes.

6   Add the sweet and sour sauce to the wok, stir well and bring to the boil. Return the meat to the wok and add the noodles, pineapple and bean sprouts. Continue to stir-fry for about 2 minutes, or until heated through, then add the spring onion and sesame oil and stir to combine. Divide among serving bowls and serve immediately.

ANOTHER IDEA

You can make this dish using the sweet and sour sauce on page 246 for a variation of flavour – it can be made in advance and stored in an airtight container in the refrigerator for up to 3 days.

Stir-fried pork with Chinese greens

PREPARATION 10 minutes   COOKING 15 minutes   SERVES 4

300 g (10 oz) pork loin steak or chops,
    trimmed and thinly sliced

¹/₄ cup (60 ml) dry sherry

1 tablespoon salt-reduced soy sauce

1 tablespoon sesame oil

250 g (8 oz) wok-ready hokkien (egg)
    noodles

1 tablespoon peanut oil

5 spring onions (scallions), thinly sliced

200 g (7 oz) snow peas (mangetout),
    trimmed and halved

350 g (12 oz) bok choy, chopped

Each serving provides
1582 kJ, 378 kcal, 25 g protein, 12 g fat
(2 g saturated fat), 38 g carbohydrate
(5 g sugars), 4 g fibre, 247 mg sodium

1 Put the pork in a bowl with the sherry, soy sauce and
1 teaspoon of the sesame oil and toss well to coat. Cover
with plastic wrap and set aside.

2 Cook the noodles according to the packet instructions, then
drain well. Toss with the remaining sesame oil and set aside.

3 Heat the peanut oil in a wok or large non-stick frying pan
over high heat. Add the pork, reserving the marinade, and
stir-fry for 3 minutes, or until the meat is lightly browned.
Remove to a plate.

4 Add the snow peas to the wok and stir-fry for 30 seconds,
then add the spring onions and bok choy and stir-fry for
a further 1 minute. Return the pork to the wok with the
reserved marinade and stir-fry for 1–2 minutes, or until
heated through and the bok choy has wilted.

5 Divide the noodles among serving plates and serve the pork
and vegetables over the top.

Sesame sausages with vegetables

PREPARATION 10 minutes   COOKING 25 minutes   SERVES 4

1   Preheat the grill (broiler) to medium. Cook the capsicums and sausages for about 20-25 minutes, turning occasionally until the sausages are cooked through and the capsicums is tender and lightly charred. Cut the capsicums into wide strips, set aside and keep warm.

2   Combine the tomato sauce and hoisin sauce in a large shallow bowl. Add the sausages and roll to coat.

3   Cover the grill rack with foil and continue grilling the sausages for 1 minute, or until the glaze is bubbling. Turn the sausages and sprinkle with the sesame seeds, then cook for a further 1 minute, or until the seeds are golden.

4   Thickly slice the sausages on the diagonal and combine with the capsicums and bok choy, tossing together to combine. Divide among serving bowls and serve immediately.

2 large red capsicums (bell peppers), halved and seeded

2 large yellow capsicums (bell peppers), halved and seeded

4 thick pork sausages

2 tablespoons tomato sauce (ketchup)

2 tablespoons hoisin sauce

3 tablespoons sesame seeds

3 heads bok choy, chopped

Each serving provides
1536 kJ, 367 kcal, 16 g protein, 28 g fat (10 g saturated fat), 14 g carbohydrate (10 g sugars), 5 g fibre, 965 mg sodium

Beef, lamb & pork

149

Chinese pork and cabbage rolls

Crunchy water chestnuts are combined with minced (ground) pork, soy sauce, fresh ginger and Chinese five-spice to make a Chinese-style filling for fresh cabbage leaves. Serve with steamed white rice and a simple salad for a quick and easy family meal.

PREPARATION 10 minutes   COOKING 20 minutes   SERVES 4 (makes 8 rolls)

1   Put the pork in a bowl with the water chestnuts, Chinese five-spice, ginger, spring onions, soy sauce, garlic and egg. Mix thoroughly with your hands until the ingredients are well combined, then divide into 8 equal portions.

2   Cut the tough stalk from the base of each cabbage leaf with a sharp knife. Place a portion of the pork mixture in the centre of each cabbage leaf, then wrap the leaf around the filling to enclose it.

3   Pour the stock into a large saucepan and bring to a simmer. Set a steamer over the pan and arrange the cabbage rolls, join side down, in an even layer. Steam the cabbage rolls for 15 minutes, or until the cabbage is tender and the rolls are firm when pressed. Remove to a plate and keep warm.

4   Add the cornflour and 2 tablespoons water to the stock and bring to the boil, then reduce the heat and simmer, stirring constantly, until slightly thickened. Stir in the chilli sauce until well combined.

5   Divide the cabbage rolls among serving bowls and spoon over some of the broth. Garnish with the extra spring onion and serve immediately with steamed rice.

HEALTHY EATING

Water chestnuts provide small amounts of potassium, iron and fibre, but their big advantage is that they contain no fat and very few kilojoules, making them a great addition to this dish.

500 g (1 lb) lean minced (ground) pork

3/4 cup (140 g) finely chopped canned water chestnuts

2 teaspoons Chinese five-spice

1 tablespoon grated fresh ginger

2 spring onions (scallions), finely chopped, plus extra, to garnish

2 tablespoons salt-reduced soy sauce

2 cloves garlic, crushed

1 egg, lightly beaten

8 large green cabbage leaves

2 cups (500 ml) salt-reduced chicken stock

2 teaspoons cornflour (cornstarch)

1 teaspoon sweet chilli sauce (see page 246), or to taste

Each serving provides
1010 kJ, 241 kcal, 32 g protein, 8 g fat
(3 g saturated fat), 10 g carbohydrate
(6 g sugars), 4 g fibre, 818 mg sodium

Chinese slow-cooked pork

Star anise, soy and ginger add wonderful flavours to this deliciously tender pork casserole, simmered with carrots and mushrooms. Rice noodles cooked in exotic, rich juices make this into a complete meal that is sure to impress.

PREPARATION 15 minutes   COOKING about 1¼ hours   SERVES 4

500 g (1 lb) lean, boneless pork loin with skin, tied firmly

1¾ cups (435 ml) salt-reduced chicken stock

2 tablespoons salt-reduced soy sauce

2 tablespoons shaoxing rice wine or dry sherry

2 tablespoons honey

2 cloves garlic, crushed

2 tablespoons grated fresh ginger

3 star anise

4 French shallots (eschalots), halved

2 large carrots, sliced

6 spring onions (scallions)

1 cup (25 g) dried Chinese mushrooms, soaked in water to rehydrate

1⅓ cups (125 g) sliced oyster mushrooms

250 g (8 oz) dried rice stick noodles

Each serving provides
2105 kJ, 503 kcal, 35 g protein, 4 g fat (1 g saturated fat), 77 g carbohydrate (17 g sugars), 4 g fibre, 833 mg sodium

1   Put the pork in a large flameproof casserole dish over high heat. Add just enough boiling water to cover and bring back to the boil, then pour off the water. Add the stock, soy sauce, rice wine, honey, garlic, ginger, star anise, shallots and carrots to the dish and bring to the boil. Thickly slice 4 of the spring onions and add to the dish. Roughly chop the drained Chinese mushrooms and add to the dish, then strain and reserve the soaking liquid.

2   Cover the dish with a lid and simmer over low heat for 40 minutes, stirring the vegetables and basting the meat occasionally until tender. Add the oyster mushrooms and continue cooking for a further 20 minutes, topping up with the reserved mushroom soaking liquid or more stock or water if necessary.

3   Finely slice the remaining spring onions into thin lengths, place in a bowl of iced water and set aside to curl. Soak the noodles according to the packet instructions, then drain well.

4   Carefully lift the pork out of the casserole dish with a slotted spoon and keep hot. Bring the juices to the boil on the stove, then add the noodles and remove the dish from the heat. Turn and stir the noodles to coat with the juices. Thinly slice the pork.

5   Divide the noodles and vegetables among serving bowls and arrange the pork over the top. Scatter over the curled spring onion and serve immediately.

ANOTHER IDEA

You can omit the noodles from this dish and simply serve the pork and vegetables on a bed of steamed rice with a little of the sauce spooned over the top for another delicious dinner idea.

Stir-fried pork with bok choy

Stir-fries do not have to be complicated, with numerous ingredients, as this simple recipe shows. Here strips of pork tenderloin are marinated then stir-fried with bok choy, allowing the flavours of the key ingredients to really shine through.

PREPARATION 15 minutes, plus 15 minutes marinating   COOKING 10 minutes   SERVES 4

1 Combine the soy sauce, cornflour, sesame oil, sugar, pepper and $1^{1}/_{2}$ tablespoons of the rice wine in a bowl. Add the pork and toss to coat. Cover with plastic wrap and set aside for at least 15 minutes.

2 Heat 1 tablespoon of the vegetable oil in a wok or large non-stick frying pan over high heat. Add the bok choy and stir-fry for about 4 minutes, or until wilted. Remove the bok choy to a plate.

3 Add the remaining oil to the wok, add the garlic and cook for about 30 seconds, then add the pork and stir-fry for about 3-4 minutes, or until the meat is cooked to your liking. Return the bok choy to the pan with the remaining rice wine and cook until heated through. Divide among serving bowls and serve immediately.

HEALTHY EATING

Bok choy, a variety of Chinese cabbage, has broad white stalks topped with large, dark green leaves. Like other dark green, leafy vegetables, it is a particularly good source of folate, and B vitamins that help to protect against heart disease.

2 tablespoons salt-reduced soy sauce

1 tablespoon cornflour (cornstarch)

1 teaspoon dark sesame oil

1 teaspoon soft brown sugar

$^{1}/_{4}$ teaspoon black pepper

$^{1}/_{4}$ cup (60 ml) shaoxing rice wine

500 g (1 lb) pork loin steak or chops, trimmed and thinly sliced

2 tablespoons vegetable oil

425 g (15 oz) bok choy, chopped

2 cloves garlic, crushed

Each serving provides
1101 kJ, 263 kcal, 29 g protein, 13 g fat (2 g saturated fat), 3 g carbohydrate (<1 g sugars), 2 g fibre, 446 mg sodium

Chinese pork with plums

PREPARATION 20 minutes   COOKING 45 minutes   SERVES 4

2 tablespoons vegetable oil

600 g (1¼ lb) lean pork loin steaks

800 g (28 oz) plums, halved, stones removed and roughly chopped

4 spring onions (scallions), sliced

750 g (1½ lb) sweet potatoes, peeled and cut into 1 cm (½ inch) cubes

¾ cup (140 g) chopped canned water chestnuts

1 tablespoon grated fresh ginger

2 cloves garlic, crushed

1 long red chilli, seeded and finely chopped (optional)

2 teaspoons sugar

1 tablespoon salt-reduced soy sauce

1 tablespoon cider vinegar

2 tablespoons shaoxing rice wine or dry sherry

¼ teaspoon Chinese five-spice

2 tablespoons chopped fresh coriander (cilantro) leaves

Each serving provides
2065 kJ, 493 kcal, 38 g protein, 13 g fat
(2 g saturated fat), 50 g carbohydrate
(29 g sugars), 10 g fibre, 295 mg sodium

1   Preheat the oven to 180°C (350°F/Gas 4). Heat the oil in a large casserole dish, add the pork and cook on both sides until lightly browned. Add the plums, spring onions, sweet potato and water chestnuts to the dish and stir well to combine.

2   Put the ginger into a small bowl with the garlic, chilli if using, sugar, soy sauce, vinegar, rice wine and the Chinese five-spice. Mix well, then spoon the mixture over the ingredients in the casserole dish. Cover and cook in the oven, stirring occasionally, for about 45 minutes, or until the meat is tender and the sauce has thickened.

3   Taste the sauce and add more sugar or vinegar if needed, depending on the flavour of the plums. Divide among serving bowls and serve immediately with the coriander sprinkled over the top.

HEALTHY EATING

Plums are a good source of vitamin C, giving them antioxidant properties and also helping to increase the absorption of iron in the body. If fresh plums are unavailable use canned instead.

Sesame pork and noodle salad

PREPARATION 20 minutes   COOKING 15 minutes   SERVES 4

1 Put the pork in a bowl with the ginger, garlic, sesame oil, soy sauce, sherry and vinegar and toss well to coat. Cover with plastic wrap and set aside.

2 Cook the noodles according to the packet instructions, then drain well. Place in a bowl with the capsicum, carrot, spring onion and bean sprouts and toss to combine.

3 Blanch the snow peas in a saucepan of boiling water for about 1 minute, or until just tender. Refresh immediately under cold water, drain well and add to the noodle salad, tossing well to combine. Set aside.

4 Heat the sunflower oil in a wok or large non-stick frying pan over high heat and stir-fry the pork for about 4–5 minutes, or until cooked to your liking.

5 Add the pork and any cooking juices to the noodle and vegetable mixture, and toss gently to combine. Divide among serving bowls and sprinkle with the toasted sesame seeds to serve.

400 g (14 oz) pork loin steaks or chops, trimmed and thinly sliced

2 teaspoons grated fresh ginger

1 large clove garlic, finely chopped

$1^1/_2$ teaspoons sesame oil

3 tablespoons salt-reduced soy sauce

2 tablespoons dry sherry

2 teaspoons rice vinegar

250 g (8 oz) wok-ready hokkien (egg) noodles

1 red capsicum (bell pepper), seeded and cut into matchsticks

1 large carrot, cut into matchsticks

6 spring onions (scallions), cut into matchsticks

$1^3/_4$ cups (150 g) bean sprouts, trimmed

150 g (5 oz) snow peas (mangetout)

1 tablespoon sunflower oil

2 tablespoons sesame seeds, toasted

Each serving provides
1749 kJ, 418 kcal, 33 g protein, 12 g fat
(2 g saturated fat), 39 g carbohydrate
(5 g sugars), 6 g fibre, 626 mg sodium

HEALTHY EATING

In the past, pork has had a reputation for being rather fatty, but this is no longer the case. Pork now contains considerably less fat, and also contains higher levels of 'good' unsaturated fat.

Asian pork salad

This Asian pork salad makes a terrific lunch idea or light dinner. You can purchase Asian barbecued pork from most Asian butchers or substitute with chicken or pork loin steak or chops, or toss in toasted peanuts or cashew nuts for added texture.

PREPARATION 15 minutes   COOKING 5 minutes   SERVES 4

100 g (3¹/₂ oz) rice vermicelli

300 g (10 oz) Asian barbecued pork, thinly sliced

100 g (3¹/₂ oz) Asian salad greens

1 red or yellow capsicum (bell pepper), halved, seeded and thinly sliced

1 tablespoon gari (pink pickled ginger), chopped (optional)

¹/₃ cup (10 g) fresh coriander (cilantro) leaves, chopped

¹/₄ cup (7 g) chopped fresh mint

100 g (3¹/₂ oz) snow peas (mangetout), trimmed and blanched (optional)

SALAD DRESSING

2 tablespoons salt-reduced soy sauce

1 tablespoon rice vinegar

2 teaspoons fresh lime juice

1 teaspoon sesame oil

1 small red chilli, seeded and finely chopped

Each serving provides
961 kJ, 230 kcal, 22 g protein, 3 g fat
(<1 g saturated fat), 25 g carbohydrate
(3 g sugars), 2 g fibre, 535 mg sodium

1 Soak the noodles according to the packet instructions. Drain well and cut into shorter lengths, if preferred.

2 To make the salad dressing, whisk together all of the ingredients in a small bowl. Set aside.

3 Combine the pork, Asian salad greens, capsicum, gari, coriander, mint and snow peas, if using, in a large bowl. Add the noodles and dressing and toss to coat. Divide among serving bowls and serve immediately.

ANOTHER IDEA

If you opt to use chicken or pork, use 350 g (12 oz) and bake in a preheated 200°C (400°F/Gas 6) oven for about 20-25 minutes, or until cooked through. Rest for 10 minutes before shredding the meat and add to the salad once cool.

Chinese roast pork

A hoisin and soy marinade adds rich colour and flavour to lean and juicy pork fillets. It makes a wonderful meal that is perfect for entertaining when served with lightly sautéed carrots and Asian greens or with noodles or steamed rice on the side.

PREPARATION 15 minutes, plus at least 2 hours marinating   COOKING 25 minutes   SERVES 4-6

1   Place the pork in a non-metallic dish and rub all over with the Chinese five-spice powder and then the crushed garlic.

2   Combine the sugar, hoisin sauce, soy sauce and rice wine in a small bowl and pour over the pork, tossing to coat. Cover with plastic wrap and refrigerate for at least 2 hours.

3   Preheat the oven to 200°C (400°F/Gas 6). Pour enough water into the base of a large roasting pan to come about 2.5 cm (1 inch) up the sides of the pan. Set a grill rack over the top and arrange the pork fillets on the rack. Cook for 25 minutes, basting the meat frequently with the leftover marinade, and turning over halfway through cooking.

4   Remove the pork from the oven and leave to rest for 15 minutes, before carving into slices and serving.

ANOTHER IDEA
While the meat is resting, make a sauce by simmering the pan juices in a saucepan for 10 minutes, or until the juices thicken to a sauce consistency, then serve alongside the meat.

2 x 350 g (12 oz) pork fillets, trimmed
1 teaspoon Chinese five-spice
2 cloves garlic, crushed
$1/3$ cup (75 g) caster (superfine) sugar
$1/2$ cup (125 ml) hoisin sauce
2 tablespoons salt-reduced soy sauce
$1^{1}/_{2}$ tablespoons shaoxing rice wine, sake or dry sherry

Each serving provides
828 kJ, 198 kcal, 16 g protein, 3 g fat
(<1 g saturated fat), 25 g carbohydrate
(23 g sugars), 3 g fibre, 750 mg sodium

Thai pork patties with coconut greens

For a lively midweek meal, try these little meat patties with vegetables, which are cooked with the typically aromatic Thai flavourings of green curry and lemongrass. Serve with steamed rice or coconut rice on the side, if desired.

PREPARATION 15 minutes   COOKING 15 minutes   SERVES 4 (makes 12 patties)

500 g (1 lb) lean minced (ground) pork
4 spring onions (scallions), finely chopped
1½ teaspoons green curry paste (see page 248)
2 teaspoons crushed lemongrass
1 egg white
2 tablespoons peanut or sunflower oil
200 g (7 oz) bok choy, chopped
2 cups (180 g) sliced oyster mushrooms
200 ml (7 fl oz) low-fat coconut milk
1 teaspoon fish sauce
1 tablespoon sesame seeds

Each serving provides
1508 kJ, 360 kcal, 31 g protein, 23 g fat (8 g saturated fat), 6 g carbohydrate (3 g sugars), 3 g fibre, 342 mg sodium

1 Put the minced pork, spring onions, curry paste, lemongrass and egg white into a large bowl and use your hands to thoroughly combine. Divide the mixture into 12 portions and mould each portion into a patty shape.

2 Heat 1 tablespoon of the peanut oil in a wok or large non-stick frying pan and cook the patties, in batches if necessary, for about 8-10 minutes, turning once, until golden brown and cooked through. Remove from the wok and keep warm.

3 Heat the remaining oil in the clean wok over high heat. Add the bok choy and mushrooms and stir-fry for 2-3 minutes, or until the bok choy has wilted. Add the coconut milk and fish sauce, bring to the boil, then reduce the heat and simmer for 1 minute.

4 Serve the Thai pork patties with the bok choy and coconut sauce on the side, sprinkled with sesame seeds.

ANOTHER IDEA

Unless you cook with lemongrass frequently, buying fresh can be wasteful; a useful alternative is a jar or tube of crushed lemongrass paste, which can be stored in the refrigerator.

Stir-fried lamb and peas

PREPARATION 15 minutes   COOKING 10 minutes   SERVES 4

2 teaspoons vegetable oil

3 spring onions (scallions), sliced

2 cloves garlic, crushed

3 teaspoons grated fresh ginger

1 red capsicum (bell pepper), halved, seeded and thinly sliced

500 g (1 lb) leg of lamb, trimmed and cut into 1 cm (¹/₂ inch) strips

500 g (1 lb) sugar snap peas or snow peas (mangetout), trimmed

¹/₂ cup (125 ml) salt-reduced chicken stock

¹/₄ cup (60 ml) chilli sauce

3 teaspoons salt-reduced soy sauce

Each serving provides
1191 kJ, 285 kcal, 33 g protein, 10 g fat
(4 g saturated fat), 14 g carbohydrate
(10 g sugars), 5 g fibre, 768 mg sodium

1   Heat the vegetable oil in a large non-stick frying pan over medium heat. Add the spring onions, garlic and ginger, and stir-fry for 3 minutes, or until the garlic is tender.

2   Add the capsicum to the pan and stir-fry for 2 minutes, or until just tender. Add the lamb and sugar snap peas and stir-fry for 4 minutes, or until the lamb is cooked through.

3   Combine the stock, chilli sauce and soy sauce in a small bowl. Pour into the pan and cook for 1 minute to heat through. Divide among serving plates and serve.

ANOTHER IDEA
You can substitute thinly sliced beef for lamb in this dish if you wish.

Mandarin and lamb stir-fry

PREPARATION 25 minutes   COOKING 10 minutes   SERVES 4

1 Combine the soy sauce, ground coriander, mandarin zest, sugar and cayenne pepper in a large bowl. Add the lamb and toss well to coat.

2 Heat 1 teaspoon of the vegetable oil in a wok or large non-stick frying pan over medium-high heat. Add the lamb and stir-fry, in batches, for 2 minutes, or until lightly browned. Remove the lamb to a plate. Reduce the heat to medium, add the remaining oil, capsicum, garlic and spring onions, and stir-fry for 4 minutes.

3 Combine the stock and cornflour in a small bowl. Add to the wok and bring to the boil. Return the lamb to the wok, add the mandarin segments and cook for 1 minute, or until the sauce has thickened slightly. Divide among serving bowls and serve immediately with the coriander sprinkled on top.

1^1/$_2$ tablespoons salt-reduced soy sauce

1 teaspoon ground coriander

2 teaspoons finely grated mandarin zest

^{1}/$_2$ teaspoon sugar

1 pinch cayenne pepper

500 g (1 lb) boneless leg of lamb, trimmed and thinly sliced

2 teaspoons vegetable oil

1 red capsicum (bell pepper), halved, seeded and chopped

3 cloves garlic, crushed

4 spring onions (scallions), thinly sliced

^{1}/$_2$ cup (125 ml) salt-reduced chicken stock

2 teaspoons cornflour (cornstarch)

4 mandarins, peeled, separated into segments, halved and seeded

2 tablespoons fresh coriander (cilantro) leaves

Each serving provides
1115 kJ, 266 kcal, 31 g protein, 10 g fat
(4 g saturated fat), 12 g carbohydrate
(11 g sugars), 3 g fibre, 686 mg sodium

Lamb with black bean sauce

Black beans impart an intense flavour to this dish, inspired by a classic Chinese recipe. If you are short on time you can use ready-made black bean sauce instead of soaking the fermented beans, although you will not enjoy the extra health benefits this way.

PREPARATION 10 minutes, plus 20 minutes soaking   COOKING 25 minutes   SERVES 4

1 If using fermented black beans, put them in a bowl, pour over enough boiling water to cover and leave to soak for 20 minutes. Drain well.

2 Heat 1 tablespoon of the peanut oil in a wok or large non-stick frying pan over high heat. Add the lamb and stir-fry for 1-2 minutes, or until lightly browned. Remove to a plate.

3 Heat the remaining oil in a clean wok and add the carrot, shallots, chilli, garlic and ginger, and stir-fry for 3-4 minutes, or until they start to brown. Add the mushrooms and stir-fry for a further 2-3 minutes.

4 Add the soy sauce, tomato paste, stock and fermented black beans or black bean sauce to the wok. Bring to the boil, then reduce the heat and simmer for 10 minutes, or until the beans are tender and the sauce has reduced slightly.

5 Return the lamb to the wok and cook for 1 minute, or until heated through. Divide the lamb among serving plates, sprinkle over the coriander and serve immediately.

HEALTHY EATING

Like most other legumes, black beans are a great source of fibre. They also have a low Glyceamic Index (GI) rating, are rich in antioxidants and contain good levels of folate and magnesium.

2 tablespoons salted, fermented black beans, or 1^1/$_2$ tablespoons black bean sauce

2 tablespoons peanut oil

500 g (1 lb) lean lamb fillets, trimmed and thinly sliced across the grain

1 large carrot, cut into matchsticks

4 French shallots (eschalots), sliced

1 long red chilli, seeded and sliced

4 cloves garlic, crushed

1 tablespoon grated fresh ginger

1 cup (90 g) sliced shiitake mushrooms

2 tablespoons salt-reduced soy sauce

1 tablespoon tomato paste (concentrated purée)

1^1/$_4$ cups (310 ml) salt-reduced lamb or chicken stock, or dry white wine

1 tablespoon chopped fresh coriander (cilantro) leaves

Each serving provides
160 kJ, 277 kcal, 28 g protein, 14 g fat (5 g saturated fat), 8 g carbohydrate (7 g sugars), 2 g fibre, 1071 mg sodium

Beef, lamb & pork

167

Fish & shellfish

Asian-style baked fish

Baked in banana leaves, these whole fish, infused with ginger, chilli and lime, are as visually spectacular as they are delicious. Despite their appearance, they are actually very quick and easy to prepare and are sure to become a regular favourite.

PREPARATION 10 minutes   COOKING 15-20 minutes   SERVES 4

4 x 400 g (14 oz) whole firm white fish, such as mackerel, tailor, snapper or bream, cleaned, skin on
4 banana leaves, trimmed (optional)
1 tablespoon sesame oil
3 limes, sliced
4 spring onions (scallions), sliced
2 tablespoons grated fresh ginger
2 long red chillies, seeded and thinly sliced
4 kaffir lime (makrut) leaves, very thinly sliced
1/3 cup (80 ml) salt-reduced soy sauce
steamed rice, to serve

Each serving provides
1610 kJ, 384 kcal, 67 g protein, 10 g fat (3 g saturated fat), 8 g carbohydrate (2 g sugars), 2 g fibre, 1010 mg sodium

1   Preheat the oven to 220°C (425°F/Gas 7). Cut three slashes in the thickest part of each side of the fish.

2   Cut the banana leaves so they are big enough to wrap each fish separately. Carefully submerge the leaves into boiling water for 30 seconds or just long enough to soften. Rinse under cold water to cool.

3   Place each fish on a blanched banana leaf. Rub 1 teaspoon of the sesame oil onto each fish, including the inside of the stomach cavity. Scatter over one-quarter of the sliced limes, the white part of the spring onions, the ginger, chilli and kaffir lime leaves under and over each fish and inside the stomach cavity. Drizzle with soy sauce and wrap each fish securely in a banana leaf. Alternatively, you can wrap the fish in baking (parchment) paper, then a square of foil, shiny side on the inside.

4   Bake the fish for 15-20 minutes, or until cooked through – when done the flesh will flake away easily when tested with a fork. Serve the fish on the banana leaves (but leaves are not eaten) or serve on plates with any juices drizzled over the top. Garnish with the remaining spring onions and serve with steamed rice.

ANOTHER IDEA
Substitute fish fillets for whole fish if you prefer. You can also add sliced lemongrass, garlic or fresh coriander (cilantro) leaves for a wonderful variation of flavour.

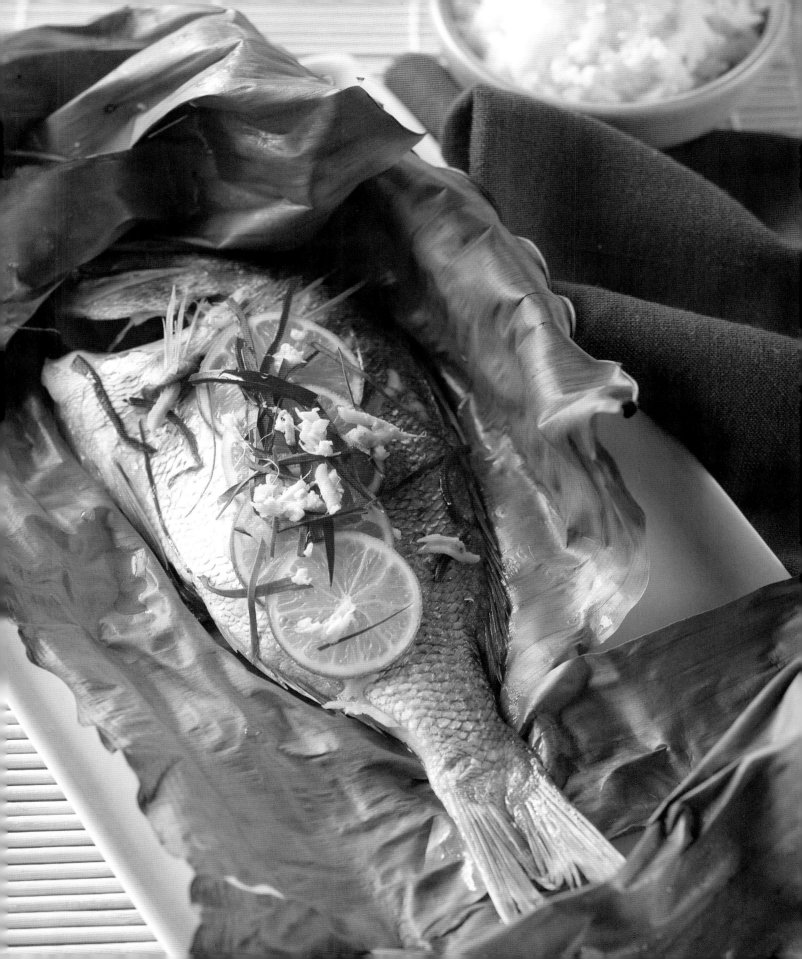

Steamed whole fish Chinese-style

A whole fish flavoured with ginger, soy sauce and sesame oil looks quite spectacular yet is easy to prepare. It is the perfect meal to serve when entertaining, perhaps with steamed rice and a side dish of crisp Asian greens or mermaid's tresses (see page 249).

PREPARATION 25 minutes   COOKING 20 minutes   SERVES 4

1   Clean and rinse the fish and pat dry with paper towels. Make three or four diagonal slashes down to the bone on each side of the fish and gently rub with the salt, inside and out. Set aside for 10 minutes.

2   Stir the soy sauce and sesame oil together in a small bowl and set aside.

3   Fill a steamer basket or wok with water so it is about 7.5 cm (3 inches) deep and bring to the boil. If using a wok, place a trivet in the bottom.

4   Rinse the salted fish under cold running water, then dry with paper towels. Place on a heatproof plate and lower into the steamer basket or wok; do not let the plate touch the water. Cover, reduce the heat to low and steam the fish gently for 15-20 minutes, or until the fish is cooked through.

5   Meanwhile, heat the peanut oil in a small frying pan and cook the chilli and ginger over high heat until softened.

6   Transfer the fish to a warmed serving dish and sprinkle with the spring onion, ginger and chilli. Pour the soy sauce and sesame oil mixture over the top, garnish with coriander sprigs and serve immediately.

ANOTHER IDEA

If you do not have a wok or steamer basket large enough to hold a whole fish, use a baking dish with a wire rack. Place the fish on its plate on the rack and cover the dish with foil, tucking it under the rim to keep the steam in.

1 whole firm white fish, such as bream or snapper, cleaned, skin on
1/2 teaspoon salt
2 tablespoons salt-reduced soy sauce
1 tablespoon sesame oil
2 tablespoons peanut or vegetable oil
1 long red chilli, seeded and thinly sliced
5 cm (2 inch) piece fresh ginger, thinly sliced
4 spring onions (scallions), thinly sliced
fresh coriander (cilantro) leaves, to garnish

Each serving provides
1388 kJ, 331 kcal, 42 g protein, 17 g fat (3 g saturated fat), 3 g carbohydrate (1 g sugars), <1 g fibre, 843 mg sodium

Smoked salmon and vegetable stir-fry

PREPARATION 15 minutes   COOKING 5 minutes   SERVES 4

1 tablespoon olive oil

1 tablespoon sesame oil

1 clove garlic, crushed

1 long green chilli, seeded and sliced

100 g (3¹/₂ oz) green beans, trimmed

100 g (3¹/₂ oz) baby carrots, trimmed

100 g (3¹/₂ oz) French shallots
    (eschalots), halved

100 g (3¹/₂ oz) asparagus spears,
    trimmed and cut into short lengths

100 ml (3¹/₂ fl oz) dry sherry

125 g (4 oz) smoked salmon, sliced

1 tablespoon salt-reduced soy sauce

¹/₂ teaspoon caster (superfine) sugar

250 g (8 oz) mixed salad leaves

Each serving provides
789 kJ, 188 kcal, 10 g protein, 11 g fat
(2 g saturated fat), 7 g carbohydrate
(6 g sugars), 3 g fibre, 777 mg sodium

1   Heat the olive oil and sesame oil in a wok or large non-stick frying pan over medium heat. Add the garlic and chilli and stir-fry for 1 minute. Add the beans and carrots and continue to stir-fry for 1–2 minutes, or until just tender.

2   Add the French shallots and asparagus to the wok and continue to stir-fry for 1 minute, then add the sherry, cover, and cook for a further 1 minute.

3   Add the smoked salmon to the wok, cover, and cook for 1 minute, then add the soy sauce and sugar and stir well to combine and heat through.

4   To serve, arrange the salad leaves on serving plates and spoon some of the salmon and vegetables over the top.

Seafood and vegetable stir-fry

PREPARATION 20 minutes   COOKING 10 minutes   SERVES 4

1   In a bowl, mix together the soy sauce, wine, cornflour, ginger and $2/3$ cup (150 ml) water, stirring until smooth. Set aside.

2   Heat the vegetable oil in a wok or large non-stick frying pan over medium-high heat. Stir-fry the garlic for about 2 minutes, or until soft. Add the prawns and stir-fry for about 3 minutes, or until they start to turn pink. Remove the prawns and garlic to a plate.

3   Add the broccoli florets to the wok and stir-fry for 2 minutes, or until they are bright green, then add the capsicum and snow peas and stir-fry for 1 minute, or until they are tender but still crisp. Return the prawns to the wok, add the baby corn, water chestnuts and spring onions. Pour in the sauce mixture and stir-fry for about 1 minute, or until the sauce thickens and boils. Serve immediately.

$1/4$ cup (60 ml) salt-reduced soy sauce

$1/4$ cup (60 ml) white wine

2 tablespoons cornflour (cornstarch)

$1^1/2$ teaspoons grated fresh ginger

1 tablespoon vegetable oil

2 cloves garlic, finely chopped

500 g (1 lb) large raw prawns (uncooked shrimp), peeled and deveined, tails left intact

4 cups (250 g) broccoli florets

1 large red capsicum (bell pepper), halved, seeded and cut into strips

1 large yellow capsicum (bell pepper), halved, seeded and cut into strips

125 g (4 oz) snow peas (mangetout)

100 g ($3^1/2$ oz) fresh or canned baby corn

$1/2$ cup (90 g) sliced canned water chestnuts

4 spring onions (scallions), sliced

Each serving provides
1120 kJ, 268 kcal, 32 g protein, 7 g fat
(1 g saturated fat), 14 g carbohydrate
(5 g sugars), 6 g fibre, 780 mg sodium

Chinese seafood soup

This light, refreshing soup has flavours that are characteristic of Chinese cookery: sesame, ginger and star anise. The dried mushrooms and shrimp paste add an intense depth to the dish; you'll find them in larger supermarkets and Asian grocery stores.

PREPARATION 15 minutes, plus 20 minutes soaking   COOKING 1¼ hours   SERVES 4

STOCK

1 tablespoon dried shrimp paste
2.5 cm (1 inch) piece fresh ginger, sliced
4 spring onions (scallions), chopped
1 star anise

SOUP

6 dried Chinese mushrooms
1 teaspoon sesame oil
1 tablespoon grated fresh ginger
2 spring onions (scallions), thinly sliced
¹/₃ cup (90 g) canned bamboo shoots,
    cut into fine matchsticks
125 g (4 oz) cooked prawns (shrimp),
    peeled and deveined
2 tablespoons salt-reduced soy sauce
2 teaspoons fish sauce
75 g (2¹/₂ oz) wok-ready thin Chinese
    egg noodles
fresh coriander (cilantro) leaves,
    to garnish

Each serving provides
631 kJ, 151 kcal, 14 g protein, 2 g fat
(<1 g saturated fat), 19 g carbohydrate
(2 g sugars), 2 g fibre, **756** mg sodium

1   To make the stock, put all of the ingredients into a large saucepan and add 6 cups (1.5 litres) water. Bring to the boil, skimming off any impurities that rise to the surface, then cover with a lid and simmer for 1 hour. Strain the stock into a bowl, discarding all of the flavourings, and set aside.

2   Rinse the dried mushrooms in cold water and put them in a bowl. Pour over enough boiling water to cover and set aside to soak for 20 minutes. Drain, then discard the stalks and thinly slice the caps.

3   Heat the sesame oil in a large saucepan over medium-high heat. Add the ginger and stir-fry for 30 seconds, then add the stock and mushrooms and bring to the boil. Reduce the heat to low and simmer for 3 minutes, then add the spring onions, bamboo shoots, prawns, soy sauce and fish sauce, stirring to combine. Bring back to the boil, then add the noodles and simmer for 2–3 minutes, or until softened. Divide the soup among serving bowls, sprinkle with coriander leaves and serve hot.

ANOTHER IDEA

You can make a vegetarian version of this soup by omitting the prawns and adding cubes of firm tofu with a handful of chopped Asian greens, baby spinach leaves or even small broccoli florets.

Seafood rice salad

A colourful, crunchy vegetable salad tossed in a tastebud-tingling, Asian-style dressing, this dish gives a great vitamin boost. Soy sauce is high in salt, so no extra seasoning is needed for the dressing. It makes the perfect lunch or light dinner during the warmer months.

PREPARATION 15 minutes   COOKING Nil   SERVES 4

1 To make the chilli dressing, put all of the ingredients into a small bowl and whisk well to combine. Set aside.

2 Put all of the salad ingredients, except the sesame seeds, into a large bowl and toss to combine. Add the chilli dressing and toss again to coat the prawns and vegetables. Divide among serving plates and sprinkle the sesame seeds on top. Serve immediately.

ANOTHER IDEA
Instead of using prawns in this dish, try it with scallops. You will need to make sure they are cleaned; cook until just opaque.

1 red capsicum (bell pepper), halved, seeded and thinly sliced

1 yellow capsicum (bell pepper), halved, seeded and thinly sliced

1 orange capsicum (bell pepper), halved, seeded and thinly sliced

4 cups (360 g) bean sprouts, trimmed

6 spring onions (scallions), thinly sliced

½ telegraph (long) cucumber, cut into matchsticks

250 g (8 oz) cooked king prawns (large shrimp), peeled and deveined, tails left intact

1¾ cups (325 g) cooked long-grain white rice

1 tablespoon sesame seeds, toasted

CHILLI DRESSING

2 tablespoons salt-reduced soy sauce

1 tablespoon sesame oil

1 tablespoon vegetable oil

2 tablespoons sherry vinegar or rice vinegar

1 tablespoon sweet chilli sauce or 1 small red chilli, seeded and finely chopped

1 tablespoon honey

2 teaspoons grated fresh ginger

Each serving provides
2180 kJ, 520 kcal, 25 g protein, 12 g fat (2 g saturated fat), 75 g carbohydrate (13 g sugars), 5 g fibre, 761 mg sodium

Asian chilli crabmeat soup

Fresh crabmeat is preferred for this recipe, as it has a better flavour and texture. However, if it is unavailable, canned crabmeat can be substituted. Crabs have both delicate white meat and stronger flavoured brown meat – both are used to great effect in this recipe.

PREPARATION 15 minutes   COOKING 15 minutes   SERVES 4

2 cups (350 g) crabmeat

6 French shallots (eschalots), roughly chopped

1 clove garlic, chopped

3 cups (750 ml) salt-reduced hot fish stock

1/3 cup (65 g) basmati rice

1 1/2 teaspoons dried red chilli flakes

2 teaspoons fish sauce

200 ml (7 fl oz) low-fat coconut milk

juice of 1 lime

3 tablespoons chopped fresh coriander (cilantro) leaves, to serve

2 spring onions (scallions), thinly sliced, to serve

Each serving provides
967 kJ, 231 kcal, 21 g protein, 7 g fat
(6 g saturated fat), 20 g carbohydrate
(2 g sugars), <1 g fibre, 745 mg sodium

1   Put any brown crabmeat, the shallots, garlic and fish stock in a food processor or blender and process until smooth.

2   Transfer the stock mixture to a saucepan over high heat and add the rice and chilli flakes. Bring to the boil, then reduce the heat to low, cover, and simmer for about 10 minutes, stirring occasionally, or until the rice is just tender.

3   Add the fish sauce, coconut milk and lime juice to the pan, stirring to combine. Add the white crabmeat and heat through gently. Season with salt and freshly ground black pepper, to taste. To serve, ladle the soup into bowls and sprinkle with the coriander and spring onions.

ANOTHER IDEA

If you have time, serve this soup with a dish of coarsely shredded or thinly sliced vegetables (such as carrot, celery, onion and cucumber). You can serve the vegetables with a sprinkling of rice vinegar or white wine vinegar, and slices of crusty bread.

Steamed fish with ginger and sesame

PREPARATION 10 minutes   COOKING 10 minutes   SERVES 4

2 tablespoons grated fresh ginger

3 cloves garlic, finely chopped

$1/2$ teaspoon finely grated lime zest

$1/2$ cup (15 g) chopped fresh coriander
    (cilantro) leaves

4 x 150 g (5 oz) skinless, boneless firm
    white fish fillets, such as flathead

$2^1/2$ teaspoons sesame oil

2 tablespoons fresh lime juice

1 teaspoon cornflour (cornstarch),
    blended with 1 tablespoon water

Each serving provides
752 kJ, 180 kcal, 32 g protein, 5 g fat
(1 g saturated fat), 3 g carbohydrate
(<1 g sugars), <1 g fibre, 148 mg sodium

1 Combine the ginger, garlic, lime zest and half of the
coriander in a small bowl. Place the fish fillets, skin-side up,
on a large heatproof plate and season first with freshly
ground black pepper then the coriander mixture. Fold the
fish fillets in half and drizzle over the sesame oil.

2 Place a cake rack in a frying pan large enough to hold the
plate and add enough water to reach just below the cake
rack. Cover the pan and bring the water to a simmer.

3 Carefully place the plate of fish on the rack over the
simmering water. Cover and steam for 5 minutes, or until
just cooked. Transfer to a serving platter and keep warm.

4 Pour the cooking liquids from the plate into a small
saucepan. Add the lime juice and $1/2$ cup (125 ml) water
and bring to the boil. Stir in the cornflour mixture and cook,
stirring continuously, until the sauce is slightly thickened.
Stir in the remaining coriander and serve on the side of
the steamed fish with grilled capsicum (bell pepper) and rice.

Teriyaki swordfish skewers

PREPARATION 15 minutes, plus 1 hour marinating   COOKING 10 minutes   SERVES 4 (makes 8)

1 Soak 8 bamboo skewers in cold water for 30 minutes, to prevent them from burning during cooking. Lightly oil a chargrill pan or barbecue hotplate to high.

2 Cut the swordfish into 24 bite-sized pieces. Mix together the marinade ingredients in a large bowl, add the fish and turn to coat. Thread the fish onto the skewers, alternating with the onion slices, capsicum and lime. Return the skewers to the marinade, cover and refrigerate for at least 1 hour, turning once.

3 Cook the skewers for 8-10 minutes, turning and basting with the marinade once during cooking – the fish should still be slightly translucent in the centre. Serve with the sweet chilli noodles, and the coriander sprinkled on top.

550 g (1¼ lb) thick swordfish steaks
4 small red onions, quartered
1 large yellow capsicum (bell pepper), halved, seeded and cut into cubes
2 limes, each cut into 8 slices
sweet chilli noodles (see page 247), to serve
2 tablespoons chopped fresh coriander (cilantro) leaves, to serve

MARINADE
¼ cup (60 ml) teriyaki marinade
1 tablespoon honey
1 teaspoon sesame oil
1 clove garlic, crushed

Each serving (2 skewers) provides
968 kJ, 231 kcal, 29 g protein, 4 g fat
(1 g saturated fat), 20 g carbohydrate
(15 g sugars), 1 g fibre, 434 mg sodium

Mixed seafood noodle broth

In China, soups are made with a lightly flavoured stock which makes them perfect not only for serving at the beginning of the meal but in between courses or dishes as well. You can partly prepare this soup ahead of time, then add the seafood, vegetables and noodles just before serving.

PREPARATION 15 minutes   COOKING 10 minutes   SERVES 6

1   Soak the noodles in boiling water according to the packet directions. Set aside until needed.

2   Heat the canola oil in a large saucepan over medium heat. Add the ginger and mushrooms and cook for about 2 minutes to soften slightly. Add the stock, sherry and soy sauce and bring to the boil.

3   Add the mixed seafood to the boiling stock, together with the bok choy, spring onions and bean sprouts. Bring back to the boil and cook for 1 minute, or until the seafood is heated through and the bok choy has wilted.

4   Add the noodles to the soup and simmer for a further 1 minute until heated through. Divide the seafood, noodles and vegetables among serving bowls and pour the broth over the top. Scatter over the coriander and serve with the chilli sauce on the side.

HEALTHY EATING

Shiitake mushrooms contain B vitamins and also provide potassium and good quantities of copper, making them a healthy addition to this broth. Oyster mushrooms are a good substitute.

50 g ($1^3/_4$ oz) thin rice noodles, broken into 10 cm (4 inch) lengths

2 teaspoons canola oil

1 tablespoon grated fresh ginger

3 cups (75 g) sliced shiitake mushrooms, stalks discarded

5 cups (1.25 litres) salt-reduced chicken stock

1 tablespoon dry sherry

2 tablespoons salt-reduced soy sauce

125 g (4 oz) cooked mixed seafood, such as prawns (shrimp), squid tubes and scallops

1 cup (75 g) shredded bok choy

4 spring onions (scallions), thinly sliced

1 cup (90 g) bean sprouts, trimmed

2 tablespoons fresh coriander (cilantro) leaves, to garnish

chilli sauce, to serve

Each serving provides
496 kJ, 119 kcal, 10 g protein, 3 g fat
(<1 g saturated fat), 12 g carbohydrate
(4 g sugars), 1 g fibre, 867 mg sodium

Noodle and squid salad

PREPARATION 15 minutes   COOKING 10 minutes   SERVES 4

3 long red chillies, seeded and finely
    chopped

1/4 teaspoon salt

1 teaspoon freshly ground black pepper

500 g (1 lb) small squid tubes, cleaned
    and halved

1 tablespoon vegetable oil

100 g (3 1/2 oz) rice vermicelli

1 small red onion, finely sliced

2 teaspoons grated fresh ginger

1 teaspoon fish sauce

2 tablespoons salt-reduced soy sauce

2 tablespoons fresh lime juice

2 tablespoons chopped fresh coriander
    (cilantro) leaves

2 teaspoons soft brown sugar

Each serving provides
1046 kJ, 250 kcal, 33 g protein, 6 g fat
(1 g saturated fat), 25 g carbohydrate
(3 g sugars), 1 g fibre, 1038 mg sodium

1   Put the chilli, salt and pepper in a bowl. Brush the squid all over with the vegetable oil. Add to bowl and toss to coat with the chilli and seasoning.

2   Soak the noodles according to the packet instructions. Drain well.

3   Put the noodles, onion, ginger, fish sauce, soy sauce, lime juice, coriander and sugar in a large bowl and toss to combine. Divide among serving plates.

4   Preheat a wok or large non-stick frying pan over high heat and cook the squid for 30 seconds on each side, or until cooked through. Divide over the noodles and serve immediately.

ANOTHER IDEA

You can add any of your favourite vegetables to this dish – why not try adding some lightly steamed bok choy or Chinese broccoli (gai larn) for some added crispness, or throw in some finely sliced carrot or zucchini (courgette).

Snow pea and seafood stir-fry

PREPARATION 10 minutes   COOKING 10 minutes   SERVES 4

1   Heat 2 teaspoons of the vegetable oil in a wok or large non-stick frying pan over medium heat. Add the snow peas, capsicum and salt and stir-fry for about 3 minutes, or until just tender. Remove to a plate.

2   Heat the remaining oil in the wok. Add the prawns, spring onions and chilli flakes and stir-fry for 1½ minutes. Add the garlic and ginger and stir-fry for 1 minute, then add the soy sauce and lemon juice and toss to combine – the prawns should just start to turn pink when done.

3   Return the snow peas and capsicum to the wok and stir-fry for just long enough to heat through, about 30 seconds. Stir in the lemon zest, divide among serving plates and serve immediately with steamed rice on the side.

ANOTHER IDEA
You can use green beans or asparagus spears instead of snow peas, or try adding a yellow squash or some canned baby corn.

1½ tablespoons vegetable oil

125 g (4 oz) snow peas (mangetout), trimmed

1 small red capsicum (bell pepper), halved, seeded and thinly sliced

¼ teaspoon salt

500 g (1 lb) raw prawns (uncooked shrimp), peeled and deveined, tails left intact

3 spring onions (scallions), finely chopped

½ teaspoon dried red chilli flakes

2 cloves garlic, crushed

1 tablespoon grated fresh ginger

2 tablespoons salt-reduced soy sauce

1 tablespoon fresh lemon juice

1 tablespoon finely grated lemon zest

Each serving provides
931 kJ, 222 kcal, 28 g protein, 9 g fat
(1 g saturated fat), 5 g carbohydrate
(3 g sugars), 2 g fibre, 709 mg sodium

Asian steamed fish

Low-fat fish and vitamin-packed vegetables are cooked using one of the most healthy of all cooking techniques – steaming. Lightly flavoured with ginger, soy sauce and white wine, this satisfying meal is so easy to prepare you will want to enjoy it all the time.

PREPARATION 15 minutes   COOKING 10 minutes   SERVES 4

750 g (1^1/$_2$ lb) skinless, boneless firm white fish fillets, such as snapper
2 tablespoons salt-reduced soy sauce
2 tablespoons white wine or sake
2 cm (^{3}/$_4$ inch) piece fresh ginger, finely sliced
2 carrots, cut into thin matchsticks
^{2}/$_3$ cup (60 g) sliced snow peas (mangetout)
^{1}/$_2$ yellow capsicum (bell pepper), seeded and cut into thin matchsticks
lemon wedges, to serve

Each serving provides
874 kJ, 209 kcal, 40 g protein, 3 g fat
(1 g saturated fat), 3 g carbohydrate
(3 g sugars), 1 g fibre, 543 mg sodium

1 Place the fish in a baking dish that will fit on a rack inside a large frying pan or in the top of a steamer basket. Combine the soy sauce and white wine or sake and pour over the fish. Top with the ginger and carrot.

2 Fill the pan with water so that it is about 2.5 cm (1 inch) deep and bring to a simmer. Place the rack or steamer basket in the pan. Place the baking dish on the rack, cover, and steam the fish for 5-6 minutes. Add the snow peas and capsicum to the dish, re-cover, and continue steaming for about 5 minutes, or until the fish flakes easily when tested with a fork and the vegetables are just tender. Divide the fish among serving plates, scatter some of the vegetables on top, and serve with lemon wedges on the side.

HEALTHY EATING

As well as being low in fat and high in protein, fish is an excellent source of omega-3 fatty acids. It is believed that eating fish regularly at least twice a week can help reduce the risk of diabetes, asthma and cardiovascular disease.

Aromatic steamed swordfish

PREPARATION 20 minutes   COOKING 20 minutes   SERVES 4

8 spring onions (scallions), thinly sliced

1²/₃ cups (200 g) thinly sliced bok choy

1 cup (100 g) sliced snow peas
(mangetout)

2 tablespoons fresh lime juice

1 tablespoon fish sauce

2 teaspoons sesame oil

4 x 150 g (5 oz) swordfish steaks, about
1 cm (¹/₂ inch) thick

1 stem lemongrass, white part only,
finely chopped

1 long red chilli, seeded and finely
chopped

1 clove garlic, finely chopped

1 tablespoon grated fresh ginger

1 kaffir lime (makrut) leaf, shredded

600 ml (21 fl oz) hot salt-reduced
vegetable stock

225 g (8 oz) mixed basmati and
wild rice

Each serving provides
1736 kJ, 415 kcal, 38 g protein, 7 g fat
(2 g saturated fat), 51 g carbohydrate
(7 g sugars), 4 g fibre, 1544 mg sodium

1 Put the spring onions, bok choy and snow peas in a bowl.
Whisk together 1 tablespoon of the lime juice with the fish
sauce and sesame oil. Sprinkle 1 tablespoon of this mixture
over the greens and toss to coat.

2 Cut out four 30 cm (12 inch) squares of baking (parchment)
paper. Arrange one-quarter of the shredded greens in the
middle of each square. Top each with a swordfish steak.

3 Reserve 1 teaspoon of the chopped lemongrass. Put the rest
in a mortar with the chilli, garlic and ginger and lightly crush
with a pestle until aromatic. Stir in the remaining lime juice
mixture, then spread this evenly over the fish. Scatter over
the shredded kaffir lime leaf, then loosely fold over each
paper to form a parcel, twisting the edges to seal. Arrange
the parcels in a steamer basket.

4 Pour the stock into a saucepan, add the reserved lemongrass, rice and remaining lime juice. Bring to the boil, then
cover and cook for 5 minutes. Place the steamer basket on
top, cover, and cook for 15 minutes, or until the fish and rice
are tender. Remove from the heat and leave to stand for a
further 2-3 minutes, or until all the stock is absorbed.

5 Carefully open the parcels, tip the juices into the rice and
gently stir to mix. Spoon the rice onto warmed plates.
Carefully transfer the fish and greens to the plates and
serve immediately.

Mixed seafood and vegetable stir-fry

PREPARATION 30 minutes COOKING 5 minutes SERVES 4

1 To prepare the squid, grasp one of the squid with one hand; with the other, pull the tentacles and the quill from inside the body. Wash the insides and remove the flaps and skin. Cut the squid in half, then gently score the inside of the flesh in a crisscross pattern (without cutting through), then slice into bite-sized pieces. To use the tentacles, cut into shorter lengths. Repeat with the remaining squid.

2 To make the sauce, combine all of the ingredients in a bowl, stirring well to combine.

3 Heat 1^1/$_2$ tablespoons of the vegetable oil in a wok or large non-stick frying pan over high heat. Add the fish and cook for 1 minute, tossing frequently. Add the prawns and squid and cook for a further 1–2 minutes, or until the prawns just start to turn pink. Transfer to a plate to keep warm.

4 Heat the remaining oil in the wok, add the ginger and garlic and stir-fry for 30 seconds. Add the broccoli and carrot and stir-fry for 1 minute, or until they are just tender. Return the seafood to the wok, add the spring onions and the sauce and stir-fry for a further 1 minute, or until the sauce thickens and the seafood is cooked through. Divide among serving bowls and serve immediately.

450 g (15^3/$_4$ oz) squid

2 tablespoons vegetable oil

500 g (1 lb) firm white fish fillets, cut into 3 cm (1^1/$_4$ inch) pieces

350 g (12 oz) raw king prawns (uncooked large shrimp), peeled and deveined, tails left intact

2 teaspoons grated fresh ginger

2 cloves garlic, chopped

1 cup (60 g) small broccoli florets

1 carrot, cut into thin matchsticks

2 spring onions (scallions), sliced

SAUCE

1 cup (250 ml) salt-reduced chicken stock

1 tablespoon oyster sauce

2 teaspoons salt-reduced soy sauce

2 teaspoons sugar

1 tablespoon cornflour (cornstarch)

Each serving provides
1806 kJ, 431 kcal, 63 g protein, 14 g fat (3 g saturated fat), 7 g carbohydrate (4 g sugars), 1 g fibre, 953 mg sodium

Fish & shellfish

Seafood and noodle stir-fry

For a quick and delicious treat, this Asian seafood stir-fry is hard to beat. It requires very little oil and the seaweed and vegetables add lots of flavour and texture. Gari, or pickled ginger, can be found in large supermarkets or Asian grocery stores.

PREPARATION 10 minutes, plus 10 minutes soaking   COOKING 15 minutes   SERVES 4

1   Mix together the lemon juice, honey and 1 tablespoon of the soy sauce in a small bowl. Pour over the scallops and prawns and set aside for about 5 minutes to marinate.

2   Place the wakame in a bowl, cover with 300 ml (10 fl oz) water and set aside for 8-10 minutes to rehydrate. Soak the noodles according to the packet instructions. Drain well and set aside.

3   Drain the scallops and prawns, reserving the marinade, and pat the seafood dry with paper towels. Heat the sunflower oil in a wok or large non-stick frying pan over high heat. Add the scallops and prawns and stir-fry for 2-3 minutes, or until the prawns just start to turn pink and the scallops are opaque. Remove to a plate.

4   Add the bean sprouts, bok choy, reserved marinade, remaining soy sauce and the gari to the wok and stir-fry for 1-2 minutes, or until the bok choy has wilted slightly. Return the scallops and prawns to the wok with the wakame and stir-fry for 1 minute, or until just heated through. Toss through the noodles to heat through, then divide among serving bowls and serve immediately.

ANOTHER IDEA

You can omit the wakame and pickled ginger from this recipe and serve with more vegetables instead. Try adding some shredded Chinese cabbage (wombok), some thinly sliced spring onions (scallions) or sliced canned water chestnuts.

juice of 1 lemon or lime

2 teaspoons honey

2 tablespoons soy sauce

200 g (7 oz) scallops, roe removed, quartered

175 g (6 oz) raw tiger prawns (uncooked large shrimp), peeled and deveined, tails left intact

10 g ($^1/_4$ oz) dried wakame seaweed

350 g (12 oz) wok-ready hokkien (egg) noodles

1 tablespoon sunflower or sesame oil

$3^1/_3$ cups (300 g) bean sprouts, trimmed

2 cups (150 g) shredded bok choy

$1^1/_2$ tablespoons gari (pink pickled ginger)

Each serving provides
1538 kJ, 367 kcal, 26 g protein, 6 g fat (1 g saturated fat), 52 g carbohydrate (5 g sugars), 6 g fibre, 667 mg sodium

Fish & shellfish

Scallops with noodles and watercress

PREPARATION 15 minutes   COOKING 20 minutes   SERVES 4

200 g (7 oz) dried thin egg noodles

300 g (10 oz) scallops, roe removed, thickly sliced

1 clove garlic, crushed

finely grated zest of 1 lemon

1 teaspoon English mustard

4 sprigs fresh tarragon

1/4 cup (60 ml) olive oil

600 g (1 1/4 lb) mixed frozen stir-fry vegetables

4 cups (140 g) watercress

Each serving provides
1532 kJ, 365 kcal, 17 g protein, 15 g fat
(2 g saturated fat), 37 g carbohydrate
(5 g sugars), 7 g fibre, 197 mg sodium

1   Soak the noodles in boiling water following the packet instructions. Drain well and set aside.

2   Put the scallops into a large bowl with the garlic, lemon zest, mustard, tarragon and 2 tablespoons of the olive oil, tossing well to coat. Set aside.

3   Heat the remaining oil in a wok or large frying pan over high heat and stir-fry the vegetables for 5 minutes, or until just tender. Add to the noodles and toss to combine. Divide among serving plates and arrange some of the watercress on the side.

4   Add the scallops and all of the marinade to the wok and cook for 2–3 minutes, turning the scallops once, until opaque. Divide the scallops among the serving plates, reserving any leftover marinade in the pan.

5   Add 1/3 cup (80 ml) boiling water to the wok and bring to the boil, stirring to lift any residue from the base. Cook for about 1 minute, or until reduced slightly, then spoon over the watercress and scallops and serve immediately.

Seafood noodle bowl

PREPARATION 15 minutes   COOKING 5 minutes   SERVES 4

1 Put the fish stock, spring onions, ginger, lemongrass and soy sauce in a wok or large non-stick frying pan and bring to the boil.

2 Add the fish to the wok and return to the boil. Add the scallops, reduce the heat to low and simmer for 1 minute.

3 Add the prawns to the wok, stirring to combine, then add the bok choy and noodles and cook for 2–3 minutes longer, or until the noodles are heated through and the fish and scallops are opaque. Divide among serving bowls, and serve immediately.

ANOTHER IDEA
Frozen fish is a great freezer standby. Thaw larger pieces of fish for about 30 minutes and then cut into bite-sized chunks. Put small pieces of frozen fish, prawns or scallops straight into the pan and add about 5 minutes to the cooking time.

3 cups (750 ml) salt-reduced fish or chicken stock

4 spring onions (scallions), chopped

1 tablespoon grated fresh ginger

1 stem lemongrass, white part only, finely chopped (optional)

2 teaspoons salt-reduced soy sauce

225 g (8 oz) skinless, boneless firm white fish fillets, such as blue-eye cod, cut into 2 cm ($^3/_4$ inch) pieces

125 g (4 oz) scallops, roe removed, thickly sliced

175 g (6 oz) cooked prawns (shrimp), peeled and deveined

1$^2/_3$ cups (200 g) shredded bok choy

300 g (10 oz) wok-ready udon (rice) noodles

Each serving provides
1062 kJ, 254 kcal, 30 g protein, 2 g fat
(<1 g saturated fat), 29 g carbohydrate
(3 g sugars), 1 g fibre, 633 mg sodium

Fish & shellfish

195

Teriyaki-glazed seafood skewers

East meets West in this intriguing salad of tiger prawns, prosciutto, zucchini (courgette) and tomato, served on skewers and marinated in a delicious glaze with a hint of citrus. Served on a bed of lettuce leaves, this makes a stylish lunch or dinner.

PREPARATION 30 minutes   COOKING 10 minutes   SERVES 4

1 tablespoon sesame oil

1 tablespoon sunflower oil

250 g (8 oz) mixed lettuce leaves, chopped

100 g (3½ oz) baby spinach leaves

4 spring onions (scallions), green part only, chopped

⅓ cup (10 g) snipped fresh chives

⅓ cup (10 g) chopped fresh flat-leaf (Italian) parsley

⅓ cup (10 g) chopped fresh coriander leaves

50 g (1¾) prosciutto slices, trimmed of excess fat

400 g (14 oz) raw tiger prawns (uncooked large shrimp), peeled and deveined

1 zucchini (courgette), thickly sliced

12 cherry tomatoes

2 tablespoons sesame seeds

1 orange, cut into wedges, to serve

GLAZE

juice of 1 large orange

2 tablespoons sake or dry sherry

1 tablespoon soft brown sugar

1½ teaspoons salt-reduced soy sauce

1 clove garlic, crushed

Each serving provides
1316 kJ, 314 kcal, 28 g protein, 16 g fat (3 g saturated fat), 11 g carbohydrate (10 g sugars), 4 g fibre, 425 mg sodium

1. To make the glaze, place all the ingredients in a small bowl and stir to dissolve the sugar. Divide the glaze into two bowls – one to use for the skewers and the other to make the salad dressing. Set aside.

2. To make the dressing, add the sesame oil and sunflower oil to one portion of the glaze and whisk to combine. Add the lettuce leaves, spinach, spring onion, chives, parsley and coriander. Toss everything together to coat. Set aside.

3. Preheat the grill (broiler) to high and line the grill tray with foil. Cut each slice of prosciutto into thirds lengthwise to make 12 long strips. Wrap a strip around each prawn, pressing so it holds firm.

4. Thread the prawns, zucchini and cherry tomatoes onto four metal skewers, alternating the ingredients evenly between each. Generously brush half of the remaining glaze over the ingredients on the skewers, then place on the grill tray.

5. Brush the skewers again with the glaze and grill for 3 minutes. Turn the skewers over and brush with the remaining glaze. Grill for a further 3 minutes, or until the prawns just start to turn pink.

6. Divide the salad among four plates. Place a skewer on each plate. Sprinkle with the sesame seeds and serve immediately with the orange wedges on the side.

ANOTHER IDEA

You can use bamboo or wooden skewers instead of the metal skewers, but be sure to soak them in water for 30 minutes to prevent them from burning during cooking.

Sesame seafood stir-fry

PREPARATION 15 minutes   COOKING 5 minutes   SERVES 4

350 g (12 oz) raw prawns (uncooked
    shrimp), peeled and deveined

1 tablespoon sesame oil

1¹/₂ tablespoons soy sauce

1 tablespoon sunflower oil

1 long red chilli, seeded and finely
    chopped

1 clove garlic, crushed

1 stem lemongrass, white part only,
    finely chopped

2 teaspoons grated fresh ginger

1 teaspoon soft brown sugar

1 tablespoon sesame seeds

2 tablespoons chopped fresh coriander
    (cilantro) leaves

quick noodles, to serve (see page 247)

sweet chilli sauce, to serve

Each serving provides
867 kJ, 207 kcal, 19 g protein, 12 g fat
(2 g saturated fat), 4 g carbohydrate
(2 g sugars), <1 g fibre, 634 mg sodium

1   Put the prawns in a bowl with the sesame oil and soy sauce,
    and toss to coat. Tip into a sieve placed over another bowl to
    catch the marinade (there will not be much).

2   Heat the sunflower oil in a wok or large non-stick frying pan
    over high heat, swirling to coat the base and side. Add the
    prawns and stir-fry for 1¹/₂ minutes. Add the chilli, garlic,
    lemongrass and ginger and stir-fry for a further 1 minute
    longer, or until the prawns just start to turn pink.

3   Remove the wok from the heat and stir in the reserved
    marinade, sugar, sesame seeds and coriander. Serve with
    the quick noodles and sweet chilli sauce on the side.

ANOTHER IDEA

These prawns make a terrific dinner served with stir-fried egg
noodles with spinach, sliced capsicum (bell pepper), mushroom
and bok choy, all cooked in a hot wok with a little vegetable stock
for flavour, until just tender.

Malaysian prawns and pineapple

PREPARATION 15 minutes   COOKING 25 minutes   SERVES 4

1   Heat the sunflower oil in a wok or large non-stick frying pan over medium heat. Add the onion and garlic and cook for about 10 minutes, or until softened and beginning to colour. Stir occasionally towards the end of the cooking time to prevent the mixture from sticking.

2   Add the chilli, cumin, white pepper, turmeric and coriander to the wok and stir to combine. Add the fish stock, fish sauce, sugar and coconut cream and stir to combine, then reduce the heat to low, cover, and simmer for 10 minutes, or until the sauce has reduced by about one-third.

3   Add the prawns to the wok and cook, uncovered, for about 3-4 minutes, or until they just start to turn pink – take care not to overcook the prawns or they will be tough.

4   Add the pineapple and spring onion to the wok and continue to cook for 1 minute, or until warmed through. Divide among serving bowls, sprinkle with the pomegranate seeds, if using, and serve with your favourite noodles or steamed rice on the side.

2 tablespoons sunflower oil

2 onions, finely chopped

2 cloves garlic, finely chopped

1 long red chilli, seeded and thinly sliced

1 teaspoon ground cumin

1 teaspoon white pepper

1 teaspoon ground turmeric

2 teaspoons ground coriander

2 cups (500 ml) salt-reduced fish stock

1½ tablespoons fish sauce

1 tablespoon soft brown sugar

¼ cup (60 ml) coconut cream

500 g (1 lb) raw tiger prawns (uncooked large shrimp), peeled and deveined, tails left intact

250 g (8 oz) fresh pineapple, peeled, cored and chopped

3 spring onions (scallions), chopped

seeds of 1 pomegranate, to serve (optional)

Each serving provides
1228 kJ, 293 kcal, 30 g protein, 13 g fat
(4 g saturated fat), 14 g carbohydrate
(12 g sugars), 4 g fibre, 1192 mg sodium

Thai sour seafood soup

This delicious soup makes a perfect first course or light main meal. It is cooked with lime, lemongrass, fresh chilli and curry paste, giving it an unmistakable Thai flavour. You can omit the prawns and use fried tofu and vegetable stock to make a vegetarian version.

PREPARATION 15 minutes   COOKING 5 minutes   SERVES 4

1 Put the stock and 3 cups (750 ml) water in a large saucepan over high heat. Add the lemongrass, kaffir lime leaves, mushroom, fish sauce and chilli and bring to the boil. Boil for 2 minutes.

2 Add the prawns, spring onions, lime juice, curry paste and sugar to the pan and cook for 2 minutes, or until the prawns just start to turn pink. When the prawns have cooked, stir through the coriander leaves, then divide among serving bowls and serve immediately.

HEALTHY EATING

Red chillies are a great source of vitamin C and contain more than ten times the beta-carotene of green chillies. You can add the seeds to the soup if you prefer a hotter flavour.

3 cups (750 ml) salt-reduced fish stock

3 stems lemongrass, white part only, crushed

5 kaffir lime (makrut) leaves

150 g (5 oz) small mushrooms, halved

$1^1/_2$ tablespoons fish sauce

4 long red chillies, seeded and thinly sliced

500 g (1 lb) medium raw prawns (uncooked shrimp), peeled and deveined, tails left intact

4 spring onions (scallions), sliced

$^1/_2$ cup (125 ml) fresh lime juice

2 teaspoons red curry paste (see page 248)

1 tablespoon soft brown sugar

1 cup (30 g) fresh coriander (cilantro) leaves

Each serving provides
825 kJ, 197 kcal, 30 g protein, 3 g fat
(<1 g saturated fat), 12 g carbohydrate
(6 g sugars), 2 g fibre, 980 mg sodium

Chinese-style rolled steamed fish

PREPARATION 20 minutes   COOKING 20 minutes   SERVES 4

1³/₄ cup (340 g) mixed long-grain and
    wild rice

600 g (1 lb 5 oz) skinless, boneless firm
    white fish fillets, such as plaice

2 tablespoons oyster sauce

¹/₂ teaspoon caster (superfine) sugar

3 cloves garlic, finely chopped

1 teaspoon grated fresh ginger

3 spring onions (scallions), thinly sliced

100 g (3¹/₂ oz) samphire, water spinach
    or other thinly sliced Asian greens

1 carrot, peeled into long strips

1 teaspoon sesame oil

Each serving provides
2066 kJ, 494 kcal, 41 g protein, 5 g fat
(1 g saturated fat), 70 g carbohydrate
(5 g sugars), 5 g fibre, 1120 mg sodium

1 Put both rices into a large saucepan with enough water to cover and bring to the boil. Reduce the heat to low and simmer for about 15 minutes, or until tender. Drain well.

2 Cut each fish fillet in half lengthwise. Arrange the strips on a clean work surface and brush over the oyster sauce. Sprinkle each fillet with a little of the sugar. Set aside half of the garlic, ginger and spring onions and scatter the remaining half over each piece of fish. Roll up the fish.

3 Place the samphire in a steamer basket and arrange the fish rolls on top. Sprinkle with the remaining garlic and ginger, and add the carrot. Cover and steam over high heat for 5-6 minutes, or until the fish is cooked through and the samphire is just tender.

4 Arrange the samphire and fish on serving plates with the carrot on top. Drizzle with the sesame oil and sprinkle with the remaining spring onions and the coriander and serve.

Scallops and mushrooms with noodles

PREPARATION 20 minutes   COOKING 25 minutes   SERVES 4

1   To make the soy and garlic baste, mix all of the ingredients together in a bowl. Remove one-third of the baste to a separate bowl to make the soy dressing and set aside.

2   To make the soy dressing, mix together the baste and all of the dressing ingredients in a bowl, stirring until smooth. Set aside until needed.

3   Cook the noodles in a saucepan of boiling water following the packet instructions. Drain well. Put the drained noodles in a bowl, add the soy dressing and toss to coat. Add the bok choy, bean sprouts, spring onion and coriander and toss well. Divide among serving plates.

4   Put the mushrooms in a shallow glass or non-reactive dish and pour over half of the remaining baste. Place the scallops in another shallow glass or non-reactive dish and brush with the remaining baste.

5   Preheat a chargrill pan or barbecue hotplate to high. Cook the mushrooms for about 8-10 minutes, or until tender, turning once; remove to a plate. Cook the scallops for about 1-2 minutes, or until opaque. Slice the mushrooms and scatter over the salad on each plate with any of the cooking juices. Add the scallops and sprinkle the nori over the top. Serve immediately.

200 g (7 oz) soba (buckwheat) noodles
1²/₃ cups (120 g) shredded bok choy or Chinese cabbage (wombok)
2 cups (180 g) bean sprouts, trimmed
4 spring onions (scallions), finely chopped
¼ cup (7 g) chopped fresh coriander (cilantro) leaves
350 g (12 oz) large flat mushrooms
250 g (8 oz) large scallops, roe removed
1 sheet nori, toasted and thinly sliced

SOY AND GARLIC BASTE

2 cloves garlic, crushed
⅓ cup (80 ml) sunflower oil
1 tablespoon salt-reduced soy sauce
2 teaspoons caster (superfine) sugar

SOY DRESSING

juice of 1 large lemon
2 teaspoons grated fresh ginger
1 tablespoon salt-reduced soy sauce
½ small red chilli, seeded and finely chopped

Each serving provides
1834 kJ, 438 kcal, 20 g protein, 20 g fat (2 g saturated fat), 43 g carbohydrate (5 g sugars), 7 g fibre, 944 mg sodium

Fish & shellfish

203

Chilli crab

This delicious crab stir-fry is made with fresh chillies and ginger and flavoured with an unforgettable tangy sauce that you will want to enjoy again and again. Served with steamed rice on the side, this dish is perfect for entertaining.

PREPARATION 10 minutes   COOKING 15 minutes   SERVES 4

4 x 300 g (10 oz) raw (uncooked) crabs, such as blue swimmer, dungeness or redrock
2 teaspoons peanut oil
2 cloves garlic, crushed
2 small red chillies, seeded and finely chopped
2 teaspoons finely grated fresh ginger
4 spring onions (scallions), thinly sliced
1/2 cup (15 g) fresh coriander (cilantro) leaves, chopped
1 teaspoon salt (optional)
1 long red chilli, seeded and thinly sliced, to garnish
steamed rice, to serve

CHILLI SAUCE
1/2 cup (125 ml) salt-reduced fish, chicken or vegetable stock
1/4 cup (60 ml) tomato sauce (ketchup)
2 tablespoons sweet chilli sauce (see page 246)
1/4 cup (60 ml) shaoxing rice wine
2 tablespoons hoisin sauce
1 tablespoon fish sauce
2 teaspoons sugar

Each serving provides
638 kJ, 153 kcal, 9 g protein, 4 g fat
(<1 g saturated fat), 18 g carbohydrate
(14 g sugars), 3 g fibre, 1057 mg sodium

1   Prepare the crabs by lifting the flap under the crab's body with your thumb and discard. On the side opposite the eyes, insert your fingers and thumb between the top and bottom shells. Pull off the top shell and discard. Remove and discard the spongy, finger-like white gills on either side of the crab's body. Cut the body into quarters.

2   To make the chilli sauce, combine all of the ingredients together in a bowl.

3   Heat the oil in a large wok over medium-high heat and stir-fry the crabs for 6-7 minutes, tossing occasionally so they cook evenly. Add the garlic, chilli and ginger, and stir-fry for 1 minute, or until fragrant. Add the chilli sauce and stir-fry for 3-4 minutes, or until the sauce boils and thickens slightly and the crabmeat turns white. Add the spring onion and coriander, reserving some for garnish. Taste and add salt if necessary.

4   Serve the crab immediately, garnished with the remaining spring onion, coriander and chilli, with steamed rice on the side.

ANOTHER IDEA

Prawns (shrimp) or crayfish could also be added to this dish as well as or instead of the crab. Prepared crabmeat could be added in addition to crabs in shells. Use a nutcracker to crack the large claws, to enable easy removal of crabmeat when serving.

Vietnamese fish salad

'Cooked' in a powerful rice and vinegar marinade, this simple yet effective salad marries the soft texture of fish with the crunch of peanuts. With fresh herbs and hot chilli as flavourings, it makes a great lunch or dinner that tastes delicious and is good for you too.

PREPARATION 20 minutes, plus 1 hour marinating   COOKING 5-7 minutes   SERVES 4

1 Cut each fish fillet in half and then slice into long thin strips. Place the fish in a large bowl and pour over 1^1/$_4$ cups (310 ml) of the vinegar, turning to coat the fish. Cover with plastic wrap and refrigerate for 1 hour.

2 Put the onion in a bowl with the sugar and salt and pour over the remaining vinegar. Stir until the sugar and salt have dissolved, then leave to soak for 30 minutes.

3 Meanwhile, crush the peanuts finely using a pestle and mortar, then dry-fry them in a wok or large non-stick frying pan over low heat for 2-3 minutes, or until they are evenly browned. Remove them from the wok and set aside.

4 Add the rice to the wok and toast it for 3-4 minutes until it is golden all over, then place it in the mortar and crush it as finely as you can.

5 Drain the onion and remove the fish from the marinade and pat them both dry with paper towels. Place the onion and fish in a large bowl and add the mint and chilli. Toss gently to combine, then sprinkle the toasted crushed peanuts and rice on top and toss again. Garnish with extra mint and chilli, if desired, and serve.

HEALTHY EATING

Fish is one of the best sources of protein as it is low in fat and also contains healthy doses of omega-3 fatty acids. Fish prepared this way, where the fish is 'cooked' during the marinating process, ensures it retains all of its nutritional benefits.

500 g (1 lb) skinless, boneless whiting fillets or other firm white fish fillets
1^3/$_4$ cups (435 ml) rice vinegar
250 g (8 oz) onions, finely sliced
1 tablespoon sugar
1 teaspoon salt
2 tablespoons raw peanuts
2 tablespoons short-grain white rice
1^1/$_2$ tablespoons finely shredded fresh mint, plus extra, to serve
1 long red chilli, seeded and finely chopped, plus extra, thinly sliced, to serve

Each serving provides
1425 kJ, 341 kcal, 30 g protein, 6 g fat (1 g saturated fat), 21 g carbohydrate (13 g sugars), 2 g fibre, 705 mg sodium

Vegetables, salads & sides

Miso soup with vegetables

This basic miso soup is super easy to prepare and wonderfully good for you. You can add just about any vegetables, making it perfect to use up leftovers in the refrigerator, or try adding some thinly sliced chicken breast or lean beef for a more substantial meal.

PREPARATION 10 minutes   COOKING 5 minutes   SERVES 4

4 cups (1 litre) dashi or salt-reduced
   vegetable stock
150 g (5 oz) silken firm tofu, cut into
   cubes
1 cup (100 g) thinly sliced shiitake
   mushrooms
8 green beans, trimmed, cut into thirds
1/4 cup (60 g) white miso paste
3 spring onions (scallions), thinly sliced
16 snow pea (mangetout) sprouts,
   trimmed

Each serving provides
175 kJ, 42 kcal, 3 g protein, 1 g fat
(<1 g saturated fat), 4 g carbohydrate
(2 g sugars), 1 g fibre, 264 mg sodium

1 Put the stock in a large saucepan over medium heat and bring to a simmer. Add the tofu, mushrooms and beans and simmer for 2-3 minutes.

2 Put the miso in a small bowl and gradually pour in 1 cup (250 ml) of the hot stock from the saucepan, stirring until the miso is dissolved. Return the miso mixture back to the pan, stirring well to combine. Add most of the spring onions, reserving some to use as a garnish.

3 Return the stock to a simmer but do not allow it to boil. Remove from the heat and divide among serving bowls. Garnish with the snow pea sprouts and remaining spring onions and serve immediately.

ANOTHER IDEA

Yellow or red miso pastes can be substituted for white; as a general rule, the darker the colour the saltier the taste. Miso paste is available from Asian grocery stores and select delicatessens and supermarkets. If using dried shiitake mushrooms, the taste is much stronger than fresh.

Pan-fried tofu and bok choy

Bok choy is an Asian cabbage that looks more like a leafy green vegetable than a typical cabbage. It contains more beta-carotene and calcium than green cabbage does, making it a terrific addition to this healthy and delicious pan-fried tofu.

PREPARATION 20 minutes   COOKING 5 minutes   SERVES 4

1   Score five narrow grooves lengthwise along each carrot, then slice each carrot into thin rounds to create flower-like shapes. Finely dice the white part of the spring onions. Slice the green part of the spring onions into thin rings. Arrange the carrots, spring onions and bok choy on serving plates.

2   Whisk 2 tablespoons of the peanut oil in a bowl with the lime juice, soy sauce, ginger, lemon zest, sugar and a little salt until well combined. Stir in the chillies, to taste, then drizzle over the salad.

3   Heat the remaining peanut oil in a wok or large non-stick frying pan over medium heat. Add the tofu and cook until golden brown on all sides. Add the peanuts and cook briefly, stirring frequently until heated through and lightly golden. Distribute the tofu and peanuts over the salad, sprinkle over the coriander and serve immediately.

ANOTHER IDEA

Tofu is available in firm, soft or silken textures and a variety of flavours – for something different you can try smoked tofu in this dish. You can use Chinese cabbage (wombok) instead bok choy.

2 carrots
4 spring onions (scallions)
2 small baby bok choy, sliced
200 g (7 oz) firm tofu, cut into cubes
2 small red chillies, seeded and finely chopped
$1/4$ cup (60 ml) peanut oil
2 tablespoons fresh lime juice
2 tablespoons salt-reduced soy sauce
$1/4$ teaspoon grated fresh ginger
$1/4$ teaspoon finely grated lemon zest
$1/4$ teaspoon soft brown sugar
3 tablespoons roasted peanuts
1 tablespoon chopped fresh coriander (cilantro) leaves, to serve

Each serving provides
846 kJ, 202 kcal, 7 g protein, 17 g fat (3 g saturated fat), 5 g carbohydrate (4 g sugars), 3 g fibre, 392 mg sodium

Vegetable salad with coconut dressing

PREPARATION 15 minutes   COOKING Nil   SERVES 4

200 g (7 oz) Chinese cabbage
   (wombok), torn into pieces
3 stalks celery, thinly sliced
2 carrots, cut into thin matchsticks
4 spring onions (scallions), thinly sliced
200 g (7 oz) fresh or canned baby corn,
   sliced

COCONUT DRESSING:
juice of 2 limes
$1/3$ cup (80 ml) low-fat coconut milk
2 tablespoons smooth peanut butter
$1/2$ teaspoon chilli sauce
1 teaspoon fish sauce or soy sauce

Each serving provides
682 kJ, 163 kcal, 6 g protein, 11 g fat
(5 g saturated fat), 11 g carbohydrate
(5 g sugars), 5 g fibre, 254 mg sodium

1   Put the cabbage, celery, carrot, spring onion and baby corn
in a salad bowl and toss well to combine.

2   To make the coconut dressing, put 2 tablespoons of the
lime juice into a screwtop jar. Add the coconut milk, peanut
butter, chilli sauce and fish sauce. Season with salt and
freshly ground black pepper and shake well to combine.
Taste and adjust with the remaining lime juice, if needed.

3   Pour the dressing over the vegetables and toss together
to combine. Serve immediately.

HEALTHY EATING

Cabbage is a cruciferous vegetable and well known for its high
nutritional value. It is rich in antioxidants, has anti-inflammatory
properties and also contains glucosinolates, all contributing to its
reputation as one of the best vegetables for cancer prevention.

Asian apple and sprout salad

PREPARATION 15 minutes   COOKING Nil   SERVES 4

1 Combine the carrot, celery, apple, bean sprouts, alfalfa sprouts and sunflower seeds in a large bowl and toss well to combine.

2 To make the lime and ginger dressing, whisk together all of the ingredients in a small bowl and season with freshly ground black pepper.

3 Just before serving, pour the dressing over the salad, toss well to coat evenly and serve.

ANOTHER IDEA

For a more substantial salad or to serve as a light main dish, you can replace the bean sprouts with sprouted green or brown lentils. You can also add $1/2$ cup (100 g) diced firm tofu that has been pan-fried in a little sunflower oil first.

1 carrot, cut into thin matchsticks

1 stalk celery, cut into thin matchsticks

1 red apple, cored, quartered and thinly sliced

1 cup (90 g) bean sprouts, trimmed

$3/4$ cup (45 g) alfalfa sprouts

$1/2$ cup (60 g) sunflower seeds

LIME AND GINGER DRESSING

1 tablespoon fresh lime juice

1 tablespoon finely chopped fresh coriander (cilantro) leaves

2 tablespoons sunflower oil

$1/2$ teaspoon sesame oil

$1/2$ teaspoon salt-reduced soy sauce

1 teaspoon grated fresh ginger

Each serving provides
934 kJ, 223 kcal, 6 g protein, 20 g fat (2 g saturated fat), 7 g carbohydrate (6 g sugars), 4 g fibre, 43 mg sodium

Steamed Asian vegetables

This recipe uses two bamboo steamer baskets so vegetables can cook more quickly; if deeply stacked, vegetables may need to be rotated during cooking. This side dish is packed with healthy vitamins. It makes a wholesome meal served with steamed rice.

PREPARATION 15 minutes   COOKING 5 minutes   SERVES 4

400 g (14 oz) carrots, cut into batons
3 cups (375 g) small cauliflower florets
3 cups (180 g) small broccoli florets
250 g (8 oz) green beans, trimmed and halved
350 g (12 oz) zucchini (courgette), cut into batons
4 baby bok choy, quartered

SWEET SOY DIPPING SAUCE
2 tablespoons kecap manis (sweet soy sauce)
1¹/₂ tablespoons oyster sauce
2 teaspoons shaoxing rice wine
1 teaspoon sesame oil

Each serving provides
533 kJ, 127 kcal, 9 g protein, 2 g fat
(<1 g saturated fat), 18 g carbohydrate
(16 g sugars), 10 g fibre, 870 mg sodium

1   To make the sweet soy dipping sauce, combine all of the ingredients in a bowl and stir well to combine. Set aside.

2   Half-fill a wok with water, cover, and bring to a boil. Scatter the carrots, cauliflower, broccoli and beans in the first steamer basket. Cover and place the steamer over the boiling water and cook for 2 minutes.

3   Scatter the zucchini and bok choy in the second steamer basket, place on top of the first steamer and cook for a further 2–3 minutes, or until all of the vegetables are just cooked. Alternatively, if only one steamer basket is available, scatter the zucchini and bok choy over the top of vegetables already cooking and steam until just tender.

4   Using a tea towel (dish towel), carefully remove the steamer baskets and divide the vegetables among serving bowls. You can either serve the sweet soy dipping sauce on the side or drizzle over the vegetables and serve immediately.

ANOTHER IDEA

You can add ginger, garlic, cubed firm tofu and other vegetables, such as asparagus, fennel and mushrooms to this dish. Substitute the dipping sauce with lemon or lime juice, tahini (ground sesame seed paste) or Asian peanut sauce (see page 247).

Tofu and vegetable stir-fry

If your family is not tempted by tofu, win them over with this Chinese-style dish. The tofu is glazed with ginger and soy, and served on a bed of garlicky noodles and crisp vegetables tossed with plum sauce. This dish is quick to make, and best of all, there's very little washing up!

PREPARATION 15 minutes   COOKING 20 minutes   SERVES 4

1   Preheat the grill (broiler). Line the grill tray with foil. Using a small knife, mark both sides of each tofu cube with a crisscross pattern and place on the foil. Fold up the edges of the foil to make a case to capture the cooking juices.

2   In a small bowl, mix together 1 tablespoon each of the soy sauce, tomato paste and canola oil. Add one-third of the garlic and all of the ginger and mix well to combine. Brush the mixture on the top and bottom of the tofu cubes and set aside while preparing the vegetables.

3   Cook the noodles according to the packet instructions. Set aside until needed.

4   Heat the remaining canola oil in a wok or large frying pan over high heat. Add the broccoli and stir-fry for 2 minutes. Add the carrots, capsicum and remaining garlic and stir-fry for 2 minutes, then stir in the stock, remaining soy sauce and tomato paste. Add the plum sauce and continue to stir-fry for 1 minute, or until the vegetables start to soften.

5   Add the noodles and bok choy to the wok, then stir in three-quarters of the spring onions and stir-fry for 2 minutes, or until the bok choy has just wilted. Remove the wok from the heat and keep warm.

6   Put the tofu under the grill and cook for 2 minutes. Turn it over and grill the other side for 1 minute. Sprinkle the sesame seeds over the top and cook for a further 1 minute.

7   Spoon the vegetables and noodles into bowls, place a piece of tofu in the centre of each and garnish with the remaining spring onions. Serve immediately.

250 g (8 oz) firm tofu, cut into large cubes
2 tablespoons salt-reduced soy sauce
2 tablespoons tomato paste (concentrated purée)
2 tablespoons canola oil
3 cloves garlic, crushed
2 teaspoons grated fresh ginger
175 g (6 oz) wok-ready thin Chinese egg noodles
200 g (7 oz) small broccoli florets, cut into small pieces
200 g (7 oz) carrots, cut into thin matchsticks
1 red capsicum (bell pepper), halved, seeded and thinly sliced
$2/3$ cup (150 ml) salt-reduced vegetable stock
$1/4$ cup (60 ml) plum sauce
200 g (7 oz) baby bok choy, thickly sliced
4 spring onions (scallions), cut into thin lengths
1 teaspoon sesame seeds (optional)

Each serving provides
1550 kJ, 370 kcal, 17 g protein, 15 g fat (2 g saturated fat), 42 g carbohydrate (16 g sugars), 8 g fibre, 878 mg sodium

Thai-style vegetable stir-fry

Ginger, chillies, garlic and spring onions provide great flavour to this simple Thai stir-fry. It is not only quick and easy to prepare but tremendously good for you as well.

PREPARATION 15 minutes   COOKING 10 minutes   SERVES 4

½ cup (125 ml) salt-reduced vegetable stock

¼ cup (60 ml) fresh lime juice

2 tablespoons salt-reduced soy sauce

2 teaspoons sugar

2 teaspoons cornflour (cornstarch)

2 tablespoons vegetable oil

4 cloves garlic, crushed

1 tablespoon grated fresh ginger

2 jalapeño chillies, seeded and finely chopped

1 red capsicum (bell pepper), halved, seeded and chopped

4 spring onions (scallions), thinly sliced

1 zucchini (courgette), diced

⅔ cup (125 g) fresh or canned baby corn

1⅔ cups (125 g) shredded Chinese cabbage (wombok)

500 g (1 lb) firm tofu, cut into cubes

Each serving provides
1175 kJ, 281 kcal, 18 g protein, 18 g fat
(2 g saturated fat), 12 g carbohydrate
(6 g sugars), 5 g fibre, 676 mg sodium

1 Whisk the stock, lime juice, soy sauce, sugar and cornflour in a small bowl until well combined and smooth.

2 Heat 2 teaspoons of the vegetable oil in a wok or large non-stick frying pan over medium-high heat. Add the garlic, ginger and chilli and stir-fry for 30 seconds. Remove from the heat and add to the stock mixture, stirring well.

3 Heat the remaining vegetable oil in the wok over high heat. Add the capsicum, spring onions and zucchini and stir-fry for about 2-3 minutes, or until just tender. Add the baby corn and cabbage and stir-fry for 1 minute, or until the cabbage wilts slightly, then add the tofu and stock mixture. Cover and simmer for 2 minutes, or until the tofu is cooked through. Divide among serving bowls and serve immediately.

ANOTHER IDEA
You can substitute Chinese broccoli (gai larn) or regular broccoli or cauliflower florets for the Chinese cabbage in this dish. You can also add your favourite mushrooms or fresh chillies instead of the jalapeños – leave the seeds in for an added kick.

Sesame asparagus and pea stir-fry

Stir-frying asparagus, rather than boiling it, preserves the water-soluble vitamins, including folate, and adds a little extra crunch. Flavoured with sesame seeds and garlic, this simple and easy side dish will complement just about any main meal.

PREPARATION 5 minutes   COOKING 15 minutes   SERVES 4

1   Toast the sesame seeds in a small non-stick frying pan over low heat, stirring frequently for about 3 minutes, or until golden. Remove to a plate.

2   Heat the olive oil in a wok or large non-stick frying pan over medium heat. Add the onion and garlic, and stir-fry for about 5 minutes, or until the onion has softened.

3   Add the asparagus and peas to the wok and stir-fry for a further 5 minutes, or until the asparagus is just tender and the peas are heated through.

4   Sprinkle the sesame seeds over the asparagus and peas, tossing well to combine. Divide among serving bowls and serve immediately.

HEALTHY EATING

Asparagus is a great source of vitamins A, C and K. It also contains B vitamins, including folate. Like most green vegetables, it is virtually fat-free, so you can eat as much as you like.

2 teaspoons sesame seeds
1 teaspoon extra virgin olive oil
$^1/_2$ cup (80 g) thinly sliced red onion
1 clove garlic, thinly sliced
750 g (1$^1/_2$ lb) asparagus, trimmed and cut into 4 cm (1$^1/_2$ inch) lengths
1 cup (155 g) fresh or frozen peas

Each serving provides
298 kJ, 71 kcal, 7 g protein, 2 g fat (<1 g saturated fat), 6 g carbohydrate (4 g sugars), 3 g fibre, 6 mg sodium

Asian greens with bacon and chestnuts

PREPARATION 15 minutes   COOKING 30 minutes   SERVES 4

Vegetables, salads & sides

30 fresh chestnuts

1¹/₂ tablespoons vegetable oil

3 slices rindless bacon (bacon strips),
   thinly sliced

2 teaspoons sesame oil

2 leeks, white part only, thinly sliced

250 g (8 oz) brussels sprouts, sliced

¹/₂ savoy cabbage, shredded

1 tablespoon salt-reduced soy sauce

¹/₄ cup (60 ml) fresh orange juice

Each serving provides
527 kJ, 126 kcal, 4g protein, 3 g fat
(1 g saturated fat), 17 g carbohydrate
(3 g sugars), 8 g fibre, 158 mg sodium

1   To prepare the chestnuts, score a cross in the base of each chestnut with a small, sharp knife. Cook in a saucepan of boiling water for 7 minutes. Remove using a slotted spoon, then, when cool enough to handle, peel off the shell and inner skin. Return the chestnuts to the pan of boiling water and simmer for 10-12 minutes, or until tender. Drain well and set aside.

2   Heat the vegetable oil in a wok or large non-stick frying pan, and cook the bacon for about 2 minutes, or until lightly browned. Remove to a plate, leaving any fat and juices in the wok.

3   Add the sesame oil to the wok and heat for a few seconds until fragrant, then add the leek and stir-fry for 30 seconds. Add the brussels sprouts and cabbage and stir-fry for 4-5 minutes, or until almost tender but still slightly crisp.

4   Return the bacon to the wok with the chestnuts, then stir in the soy sauce and orange juice. Cook for a further 2 minutes to heat everything through. Season to taste with freshly ground black pepper. Divide among serving bowls and serve immediately.

Vegetable stir-fry with garlic sauce

PREPARATION 15 minutes   COOKING 12 minutes   SERVES 4

1. Combine $^1/_4$ cup (60 ml) of the stock in a bowl with the soy sauce, cornflour and chilli powder. Stir until smooth, then set aside.

2. Heat the peanut oil in a wok or large non-stick frying pan over high heat. Add the ginger and garlic and stir-fry for about 1 minute, or until fragrant. Remove to a plate.

3. Add the broccoli to the wok and stir-fry for 4 minutes, or until it begins to soften. Remove to a plate.

4. Add the corn, capsicum and water chestnuts and stir-fry for 3 minutes, or until they begin to soften. Return the broccoli to the wok and pour in the remaining stock. Cover and cook for 3 minutes, or until the vegetables are tender. Add the cornflour mixture, return the ginger and garlic to the wok and stir-fry for about 1 minute, or until the sauce thickens. Sprinkle the sesame seeds over the vegetables, divide among serving bowls and serve immediately.

$1^1/_2$ cups (375 ml) salt-reduced chicken stock

2 tablespoons salt-reduced soy sauce

2 tablespoons cornflour (cornstarch)

$^1/_2$ teaspoon chilli powder

$1^1/_2$ teaspoons peanut or vegetable oil

2 cloves garlic, crushed

3 tablespoons grated fresh ginger

2 cups (120 g) small broccoli florets

2 cups (360 g) fresh or canned baby corn

1 large red capsicum (bell pepper), halved, seeded and thinly sliced

$1^1/_4$ cups (215 g) sliced water chestnuts

1 tablespoon sesame seeds, toasted, to garnish

Each serving provides
244 kJ, 58 kcal, 3 g protein, 2 g fat
(<1 g saturated fat), 8 g carbohydrate
(2 g sugars), 2 g fibre, 282 mg sodium

Mushroom vegetable stir-fry

Stir-frying really makes the most of vegetables, retaining their colour, flavour and texture. The best thing about this dish is that you can use up any vegetables in the refrigerator and turn them into a tasty and nutritious side dish or light meal served with noodles.

PREPARATION 10-15 minutes   COOKING 7 minutes   SERVES 4

1½ tablespoons salt-reduced soy sauce

1½ tablespoons dry sherry

1 tablespoon honey

2 tablespoons salt-reduced vegetable stock

2 tablespoons vegetable oil

150 g (5 oz) carrots, cut into batons

200 g (7 oz) red capsicum (bell pepper), halved, seeded and sliced

200 g (7 oz) yellow capsicum (bell pepper), halved, seeded and sliced

150 g (5 oz) button mushrooms, halved

1 clove garlic, crushed

2 teaspoons grated fresh ginger

2 teaspoons sesame oil

Each serving provides
806 kJ, 192 kcal, 6 g protein, 12 g fat (2 g saturated fat), 12 g carbohydrate (11 g sugars), 1 g fibre, 605 mg sodium

1   Put the soy sauce, sherry, honey and stock in a small bowl. Stir together until combined and set aside until needed.

2   Heat the vegetable oil in a wok or large non-stick frying pan over high heat. Add the carrot and stir-fry for 30 seconds. Pour in 1-2 tablespoons of water, cover, and cook for about 2 minutes, or until the carrot starts to soften.

3   Add the capsicums, mushrooms, garlic and ginger, and stir-fry for about 2 minutes, or until they are almost tender.

4   Pour in the sauce and stir-fry for 1 minute until all the vegetables are coated in the sauce. Transfer to a serving platter, sprinkle with sesame oil, and serve immediately.

ANOTHER IDEA

You can add almost any vegetable to this dish – try celery, green beans, snow peas (mangetout) or any leafy Asian greens. You can also add cashew nuts, water chestnuts or even bamboo shoots for extra crunch. Add the leafy vegetables towards the end of cooking, and cook until just wilted.

Mushroom and tofu stir-fry

Mushrooms and tofu are favoured by many vegetarians as a nutritious meat alternative. You can use any mushrooms in this tasty stir-fry – the more variety the better. Look for those that are firm, plump and clean for optimum freshness.

PREPARATION 10 minutes COOKING 15 minutes SERVES 4

1 Combine the soy sauce, sugar, cornflour and $1/2$ cup (125 ml) water in a small bowl, stirring well. Set aside until needed.

2 Heat 2 teaspoons of the olive oil in a wok or large non-stick frying pan over medium heat. Add the spring onions, ginger and garlic and stir-fry for 1 minute, or until tender.

3 Add the shiitake and button mushrooms to the wok with $1/2$ cup (125 ml) water. Cover and cook, stirring occasionally, for 5 minutes, or until all of the water has been absorbed and the mushrooms are tender. Remove to a plate.

4 Heat the remaining olive oil in the wok. Add the bok choy and stir-fry for 5 minutes, or until tender. Return the mushroom mixture to the wok with the tofu, tossing to combine. Stir in the soy sauce mixture and stir-fry for a further 2 minutes, or until the tofu is heated through and the vegetables are coated in the sauce.

HEALTHY EATING
Shiitake mushrooms have long been used for medicinal purposes and are available from most supermarkets, either fresh or dried. They are a good source of iron, vitamin C, protein and dietary fibre, making them an excellent addition to any stir-fry.

2 tablespoons salt-reduced soy sauce

1 tablespoon dark brown sugar

$1^1/2$ teaspoons cornflour (cornstarch)

1 tablespoon olive oil

4 spring onions (scallions), thinly sliced

2 tablespoons grated fresh ginger

3 cloves garlic, crushed

250 g (8 oz) fresh shiitake mushrooms, stems removed and caps quartered

250 g (8 oz) button mushrooms, halved

1 large bok choy, cut into eighths

400 g (14 oz) firm tofu, cut into cubes

Each serving provides
940 kJ, 224 kcal, 16 g protein, 12 g fat (2 g saturated fat), 12 g carbohydrate (8 g sugars), 5 g fibre, 387 mg sodium

Tamarind vegetables and cashews

PREPARATION 15 minutes   COOKING 8 minutes   SERVES 4

1 tablespoon sunflower oil

$^{1}/_{3}$ cup (50 g) unsalted cashew nuts

200 g (7 oz) sugar snap peas

1 cup (180 g) fresh or canned baby corn

1 red capsicum (bell pepper), halved,
    seeded and thinly sliced

$2^{2}/_{3}$ cups (200 g) shredded bok choy

stir-fry noodles (see page 247), to serve

TAMARIND SAUCE

1 tablespoon tamarind concentrate

2 tablespoons salt-reduced soy sauce

2 teaspoons grated fresh ginger

1 teaspoon cornflour (cornstarch)

2 tablespoons dry sherry

Each serving provides
2229 kJ, 532 kcal, 31 g protein, 19 g fat
(3 g saturated fat), 69 g carbohydrate
(7 g sugars), 7 g fibre, 776 mg sodium

1   To make the tamarind sauce, put all of the ingredients in a bowl with 2 tablespoons water. Stir well to combine, then set aside until needed.

2   Heat the sunflower oil in a wok or large frying pan and add the cashew nuts. Cook for 1 minute, or until golden. Remove from the pan and drain on paper towels.

3   Add the sugarsnap peas, baby corn and capsicum to the wok and stir-fry over high heat for 2–3 minutes, or until the vegetables begin to soften. Pour in the tamarind sauce and add the bok choy. Stir-fry for about 30 seconds, then cover and simmer for 2 minutes.

4   Transfer the vegetables to a serving dish, scatter the cashew nuts over the top and serve the vegetables with the stir-fry noodles.

Lemon asparagus and crunchy greens

PREPARATION 10 minutes COOKING 5 minutes SERVES 4

1   Heat the oil in a wok or large non-stick frying pan over medium-high heat. Add the asparagus, snow peas, spring onion, salt and pepper, and stir-fry for about 2–3 minutes, or until the vegetables are just tender.

2   Add the garlic, lemon zest and parsley to the wok and stir-fry for a further 1 minute to combine and heat through. Serve immediately.

1 tablespoon olive oil

500 g (1 lb) asparagus, trimmed and sliced into 5 cm (2 inch) lengths

125 g (4 oz) snow peas (mangetout), trimmed

4 spring onions (scallions), thinly sliced

1/4 teaspoon salt

1/4 teaspoon freshly ground black pepper

1 clove garlic, crushed

1 teaspoon grated lemon zest

2 tablespoons finely chopped flat-leaf parsley

Each serving provides
339 kJ, 81 kcal, 5 g protein, 5 g fat
(1 g saturated fat), 5 g carbohydrate
(4 g sugars), 4 g fibre, 160 mg sodium

Sweet and sour tofu with vegetables

This delicious Asian-style tofu with vegetables can be served on its own as a side dish or as a light lunch over brown rice or noodles to make a more substantial main meal. Full of protein and fibre, this meal is very quick to prepare and very good for you.

PREPARATION 15 minutes   COOKING 7 minutes   SERVES 4

2 tablespoons salt-reduced soy sauce

2 tablespoons fresh lime juice

2 teaspoons sugar

4 spring onions (scallions), thinly sliced

4 cups (300 g) shredded Chinese cabbage (wombok)

1 zucchini (courgette), sliced

1 red capsicum (bell pepper), halved, seeded and finely chopped

1 cup (260 g) canned pineapple pieces, drained

375 g ($^3/_4$ lb) firm tofu, cut into cubes

1 tablespoon grated, fresh ginger

$^1/_8$ teaspoon cayenne pepper

Each serving provides
733 kJ, 175 kcal, 14 g protein, 7 g fat
(1 g saturated fat), 15 g carbohydrate
(12 g sugars), 5 g fibre, 388 mg sodium

1   Put the soy sauce, lime juice, sugar and $^1/_4$ cup (60 ml) hot water in a saucepan and bring to the boil. Add the spring onion, cabbage, zucchini and capsicum, then reduce the heat to low and simmer, covered, for 4 minutes, or until the vegetables are just tender.

2   Add the pineapple, tofu, ginger and cayenne pepper to the pan, cover, and continue to simmer for about 3 minutes, gently stirring from time to time until the tofu is cooked through. Divide among serving bowls and serve immediately.

ANOTHER IDEA

Simple braises such as this one are perfect for weeknight dining as you can add whatever vegetables you have in the refrigerator. Try adding a variety of mushrooms, snow peas (mangetout), green beans or any Asian leafy greens for good effect.

Bok choy with chilli sesame dressing

PREPARATION 10 minutes   COOKING 1 minute   SERVES 4

1 tablespoon grated fresh ginger
2 long red chillies, thinly sliced
2 cloves garlic, finely chopped
1 tablespoon sesame oil
1 tablespoon mirin (Japanese rice wine)
1 tablespoon salt-reduced soy sauce
1 teaspoon sugar
500 g (1 lb) baby bok choy
2 tablespoons sesame seeds, toasted

Each serving provides
259 kJ, 62 kcal, 3 g protein, 16 g fat
(2 g saturated fat), 4 g carbohydrate
(3 g sugars), 3 g fibre, 346 mg sodium

1   Combine the ginger, chilli, garlic, sesame oil, mirin, soy sauce and sugar in a small bowl and stir well to combine.

2   Blanch the whole bok choys in boiling water in a large saucepan for 1 minute, then drain well and place on a serving plate. Drizzle with the dressing, then sprinkle with the sesame seeds and serve immediately.

HEALTHY EATING

The capsaicin found in chillies gives them their intense flavour, or heat. Capsaicin can be beneficial to help clear congested nasal and lung passageways and can also help boost immunity.

Stir-fried tofu with vegetables

PREPARATION 15 minutes, plus 1 hour marinating   COOKING 10 minutes   SERVES 4

1 Combine the soy sauce, brown sugar, ginger and a pinch of salt in a shallow bowl. Add the tofu, cut-side down, cover and set aside for 1 hour to marinate. Remove the tofu, reserving the marinade, then cut the tofu into 3 cm (1¼ inch) chunks. Stir the stock and cornflour into the reserved marinade.

2 Heat the vegetable oil in a wok or large non-stick frying pan over medium heat. Add the capsicum, beans, carrots, garlic and spring onions and cook for 5 minutes, or until the capsicum is tender. Add the marinade and tofu and bring to mixture to the boil. Reduce the heat to low and simmer for about 4 minutes, or until the sauce is slightly thickened and the tofu is heated through. Serve immediately.

2 tablespoons salt-reduced soy sauce

1 tablespoon soft brown sugar

2 teaspoons grated fresh ginger

500 g (1 lb) firm tofu, cut into large rectangles, about 3 cm (1¼ inch) thick

¾ cup (180 ml) salt-reduced chicken stock

2 teaspoons cornflour (cornstarch)

3 teaspoons vegetable oil

1 large red capsicum (bell pepper), halved, seeded and thinly sliced

200 g (7 oz) green beans, cut into 5 cm (2 inch) lengths

2 carrots, thinly sliced

4 cloves garlic, crushed

2 spring onions (scallions), thinly sliced

Each serving provides
926 kJ, 230 kcal, 18 g protein, 12 g fat
(2 g saturated fat), 12 g carbohydrate
(8 g sugars), 6 g fibre, 642 mg sodium

Vietnamese rice paper rolls

These rice paper rolls are served cold and can be prepared in advance, making them a good option for entertaining as all the work has already been done. Filled with prawns, noodles, vegetables and mint, this dish is evocative of the flavours of Vietnamese cooking.

PREPARATION 15 minutes   COOKING Nil   SERVES 4 (makes 16 rolls)

1   Soak the noodles according to the packet instructions. Drain well and toss in a bowl with the soy sauce and sesame oil.

2   To make the nuoc cham dipping sauce, put all of the ingredients in a bowl with $1/4$ cup (60 ml) water and stir well to combine. Set aside.

3   Pour warm water into a separate shallow bowl. Working with one round of rice paper at a time, dip it into the water for about 20-30 seconds, or until it softens, then drain on paper towels. Lay on a clean work surface and place the mint and then some noodles in the lower third of the rice paper. Top with a prawn half, some lettuce, carrot, cucumber, bean sprouts and spring onion. Fold over one end, then fold over two sides to cover the filling and neatly roll up to enclose the filling and make a neat log.

4   Repeat with the remaining wrappers, noodles and vegetables to make 16 rolls in total. Serve with the nuoc cham dipping sauce on the side.

ANOTHER IDEA
Thin slices of cooked Chinese barbecued pork, chicken, sashimi tuna or salmon, or even marinated tofu can be added to these rolls. You can also vary the vegetables as desired or add sliced bamboo shoots or water chestnuts.

75 g ($2^{1}/_2$ oz) rice vermicelli

1 tablespoon salt-reduced soy sauce

$1/2$ teaspoon sesame oil

16 x 15 cm (6 inch) round rice paper wrappers

1 cup (30 g) fresh Vietnamese mint or coriander (cilantro) leaves

8 cooked prawns (shrimp), peeled, deveined and halved lengthwise

$1/4$ iceberg lettuce, finely shredded

1 small carrot, grated

1 small Lebanese (short) cucumber, seeded and cut into thin matchsticks

2 cups (180 g) bean sprouts, trimmed

8 spring onions (scallions), green part only, halved

NUOC CHAM DIPPING SAUCE

$1/4$ cup (60 ml) fresh lime juice

$1/4$ cup (60 ml) fish sauce

2 tablespoons sugar

1 red birdseye (Thai) chilli, seeded and finely chopped

1 clove garlic, crushed

Each serving (4 rolls) provides
1568 kJ, 375 kcal, 18 g protein, 2 g fat
(<1 g saturated fat), 70 g carbohydrate
(14 g sugars), 4 g fibre, 1856 mg sodium

Asian vegetables with oyster sauce

Stir-fries are excellent for week-night meals as they are quick to prepare and most of the ingredients are already in the pantry. Enhanced with fresh lime juice, soy sauce and oyster sauce, these vegetables are also terrific served with noodles or steamed rice.

PREPARATION 15 minutes   COOKING 5 minutes   SERVES 8

1 tablespoon salt-reduced soy sauce

1 tablespoon oyster sauce

2 tablespoons fresh lime juice

1 tablespoon sugar

2 tablespoons vegetable oil

4 cloves garlic, crushed

2 jalapeño chillies, seeded and thinly sliced

3 spring onions (scallions), thinly sliced

1 red capsicum (bell pepper), halved, seeded and chopped

125 g (4 oz) snow peas (mangetout), trimmed

1 lady finger (Lebanese) eggplant (aubergine), cut into small cubes

125 g (4 oz) mushrooms, stems removed and caps quartered

1 tablespoon grated fresh ginger

3 small baby bok choy, cores removed and thinly sliced

1/2 cup (15 g) finely chopped basil

Each serving provides
310 kJ, 74 kcal, 2 g protein, 5 g fat
(1 g saturated fat), 6 g carbohydrate
(4 g sugars), 2 g fibre, 293 mg sodium

1 Put the soy sauce, oyster sauce, lime juice and sugar in a small bowl and stir well to combine. Set aside.

2 Heat the vegetable oil in a wok or large non-stick frying pan over medium-high heat. Add the garlic and chilli and stir-fry for 30 seconds, then add the spring onions, capsicum, snow peas, eggplant, mushrooms and ginger and stir-fry for about 2 minutes, or until the vegetables start to soften.

3 Add the bok choy to the wok and stir-fry for 1 minute, or until it wilts. Add the soy sauce mixture and stir-fry for 1 minute, or until all the vegetables are just tender. Stir in the basil until just combined, then divide among serving bowls and serve immediately.

ANOTHER IDEA

You can add broccoli florets, diced carrots, radishes, celery or even baby corn to this dish for additional flavour and texture. The more finely cut the vegetables, the more quickly they will cook.

Grilled marinated tofu

PREPARATION 10 minutes, plus 2 hours draining and 3 hours marinating   COOKING 10 minutes   SERVES 4

500 g (1 lb) firm tofu, cut into large
     rectangles, about 3 cm (1¹/4 inch)
     thick
¹/4 cup (60 ml) salt-reduced soy sauce
2 tablespoons fresh lemon juice
1 tablespoon dark brown sugar
2 teaspoons sesame oil
1 tablespoon sesame seeds, toasted
4 spring onions (scallions), thinly sliced

Each serving provides
782 kJ, 187 kcal, 16 g protein, 11 g fat
(2 g saturated fat), 6 g carbohydrate
(5 g sugars), 3 g fibre, 566 mg sodium

1   Cover the tofu slices with paper towels on a cutting board.
     Place another cutting board on top and weight it with a
     heavy pan or a couple of cans. Let it drain on an angle for
     about 2 hours to remove any excess moisture.

2   In a shallow container large enough to hold the tofu in a
     single layer, whisk together the soy sauce, lemon juice, sugar
     and sesame oil. Add the pressed tofu, turning to coat, then
     cover and refrigerate for 3 hours.

3   Preheat a chargrill pan or barbecue hotplate to medium.
     Remove the tofu from the marinade, reserving the
     marinade. Place the tofu on the grill tray and cook for
     5 minutes on each side, or until golden.

4   To serve, cut each piece of tofu into four triangles and
     sprinkle with the sesame seeds, spring onions and any
     leftover marinade.

Chinese cabbage with ginger

PREPARATION 10 minutes   COOKING 5 minutes   SERVES 4

1   Heat the vegetable oil in a wok or large non-stick frying pan over high heat. Add the ginger and stir-fry for 30 seconds. Add the cabbage and stir-fry for 2 minutes, or until it starts to soften.

2   Add the salt and stock to the wok, cover, and cook until almost all of the cabbage has wilted, about 2 minutes. Remove the wok from the heat and leave to stand, covered, for a further 1 minute. Sprinkle the peanuts over the top of the cabbage and serve immediately.

1 tablespoon vegetable oil

1 tablespoon grated fresh ginger

6 cups (450 g) coarsely chopped Chinese cabbage (wombok) or bok choy

$1/4$ teaspoon salt

$1/4$ cup (60 ml) salt-reduced chicken or vegetable stock

1 tablespoon chopped roasted peanuts

Each serving provides
328 kJ, 78 kcal, 2 g protein, 6 g fat (1 g saturated fat), 4 g carbohydrate (2 g sugars), 2 g fibre, 200 mg sodium

Tofu satay skewers

PREPARATION 30 minutes, plus 30 minutes soaking   COOKING 15 minutes   SERVES 4

8 fresh or canned baby corn
1/2 telegraph (long) cucumber
3 1/2 cups (315 g) bean sprouts, trimmed
2 tablespoons unsalted peanuts
400 g (14 oz) firm tofu, cut into cubes
1 eggplant (aubergine), cut into cubes
1 red onion, chopped into cubes

SATAY SAUCE

1/3 cup (90 g) salt-reduced crunchy
    peanut butter
1 teaspoon salt-reduced soy sauce
1 teaspoon honey
1 teaspoon rice vinegar
1 clove garlic
1 spring onion (scallion), chopped
1/3 cup (80 ml) low-fat coconut milk
1 tablespoon sweet chilli sauce (see
    page 246)

Each serving provides
1555 kJ, 371 kcal, 22 g protein, 24 g fat
(6 g saturated fat), 15 g carbohydrate
(9 g sugars), 8 g fibre, 289 mg sodium

1   Soak 12 bamboo skewers in cold water for about 30 minutes to prevent them from burning during cooking.

2   To make the satay sauce, combine all of the ingredients in a blender or food processor and blend or process to make a thick, almost smooth sauce.

3   Blanch the fresh baby corn cobs in a saucepan of boiling water for 2–3 minutes. Refresh immediately under cold running water and drain well. Cut the cucumber into thin matchsticks. Arrange the bean sprouts, cucumber and corn on a large platter and scatter the peanuts over the top. Set aside.

4   Preheat a grill (broiler) to high; line the grill tray with foil. Thread the tofu, eggplant and onion onto the soaked skewers, spacing the pieces slightly apart. Place on the prepared grill tray and brush with some of the satay sauce. Cook for 8–10 minutes, turning the skewers frequently and brushing with the satay sauce until cooked through. Gently heat the remaining satay sauce in a small saucepan.

5   Arrange the tofu skewers on top of the salad, spoon the warm satay sauce over the top and serve immediately.

Soy-dressed green beans

PREPARATION 5 minutes   COOKING 3 minutes   SERVES 4

1 Put the garlic, ginger, soy sauce and sugar in a small bowl and stir until the sugar dissolves.

2 Blanch the green beans in a saucepan of boiling water with a pinch of salt, for 3 minutes, or until tender but still a little crisp. Drain well, then toss with the soy sauce dressing and serve immediately.

ANOTHER IDEA

You can use any seasonal vegetables in this dish – the light dressing will perfectly complement most fresh produce. Substitute sliced carrots, runner beans or fresh baby corn, adjusting the cooking time as needed until just tender.

2 cloves garlic, finely chopped

$1/2$ teaspoon grated fresh ginger

2 tablespoons salt-reduced soy sauce

$1/2$ teaspoon sugar

500 g (1 lb) green beans, trimmed and halved

Each serving provides
146 kJ, 35 kcal, 4 g protein, <1 g fat
(<1 g saturated fat), 4 g carbohydrate
(2 g sugars), 4 g fibre, 372 mg sodium

To finish a meal

There is nothing quite like something sweet or refreshing to finish a spicy meal, even if it just means cleansing the palate with a revitalising tea. Asian desserts can be as simple as fresh fruit or a cool, palate-cleansing sorbet, both low in fat.

Any fresh fruit, such as watermelon, rockmelon, honeydew, mango or banana, can be used to great effect as a stand-alone dessert but should be as fresh as possible, cut into manageable pieces if necessary, and beautifully presented. Canned fruit, such as lychees, could be substituted if fresh are unavailable. Drain them well and serve chilled, with low-fat cream or ice cream.

When cooking popular sticky (glutinous) white or black rice desserts, simmer in low-fat coconut milk instead of coconut cream, sweetened to taste – this will reduce the fat but not the flavour. A very simple option is to sweeten coconut milk with a little grated palm sugar and stir to dissolve over high heat. Once thickened, pour just enough over some steamed long-grain white rice until just coated, then fluff with a fork and serve with slices of fresh mango.

Teas

Asian meals are often accompanied by soothing green tea. Why not try other 'teas' made from infusions of fresh flavours, such as lemongrass, ginger or kaffir lime (makrut) leaves? Instead of discarding the green top of a lemongrass stem, bruise it first with the knife handle or meat mallet, cover with boiling water, adding a little sugar or honey, to taste. Infuse for 5 minutes, strain and drink the tea hot or refrigerate and serve chilled with ice cubes. Sliced fresh ginger, coarsely crushed or chopped kaffir lime or lemon myrtle leaves could also be used. These ingredients make a very refreshing drink.

You can also use the infused teas, sweetened to taste, to gently poach fruit such as peeled and halved Bosc or Corella pears. Serve warm or chilled, sprinkled with a little chopped glacé ginger and roasted almonds.

Basic recipes

These popular recipes are widely used in Asian cooking. They can be used within main dishes as directed, added to meats or vegetables for flavour and variation, or served on the side.

SWEET AND SOUR SAUCE

$1/2$ Lebanese (short) cucumber, peeled, seeded and sliced
1 teaspoon salt
$1/4$ cup (60 ml) plum sauce
2 tablespoons malt vinegar
1 tablespoon tomato sauce (ketchup)
1 teaspoon sugar
1 tablespoon vegetable oil
$1/2$ large onion, sliced

Put the cucumber in a bowl and sprinkle over the salt; set aside for 1 hour. Squeeze the cucumber to remove as much moisture as possible, then set aside until needed. Put the plum sauce, vinegar, tomato sauce and sugar in a saucepan with 150 ml (5 fl oz) water and bring to a simmer. Heat the vegetable oil in a separate frying pan or wok over high heat and cook the onion until just starting to brown. Add the cucumber and stir rapidly for 1-2 minutes. Add to the simmering sauce and cook for 1-2 minutes, stirring to combine. This sauce can then be combined with other ingredients, such as chicken, pork or seafood, to make a superb sweet and sour dish.
MAKES: $3/4$ cup (180 ml)

VARIATIONS

● To give a sharper taste to the sauce, use Chinese lemon sauce (a bottled sauce that can be found in Asian supermarkets and some speciality food stores) instead of plum sauce.
● Omit the tomato sauce but add a skinned and quartered tomato. Omit the cucumber and substitute a small can of drained pineapple chunks.
● Substitute the onion with 2 spring onions (scallions), cut into 2.5 cm (1 inch) lengths.

ASIAN DIPPING SAUCE

$3/4$ cup (180 ml) salt-reduced soy sauce
$1/2$ cup (125 ml) sake or dry sherry
2 spring onions (scallions), finely chopped
$1/4$ cup (50 g) grated fresh ginger
2 teaspoons dark sesame oil
2 cloves garlic, crushed

Combine all of the ingredients in a bowl. Cover with plastic wrap and refrigerate for at least 2 hours or overnight. Serve with spring rolls, won tons or drizzled over steamed Asian greens.
MAKES: 1 cup (250 ml)

SWEET CHILLI SAUCE

1 long red chilli, seeded and thinly sliced
2 teaspoons arrowroot powder
$1/3$ cup (80 ml) fresh lime juice
2 tablespoons rice vinegar
1 tablespoon soft brown sugar
2 teaspoons fish sauce

Put the chilli and arrowroot in a small saucepan over medium heat. Slowly stir in the lime juice, vinegar, sugar and fish sauce until well combined. Bring to the boil, and continue stirring until thickened. Remove from the heat and leave to cool to room temperature. Use immediately, or store in an airtight container for up to 4 days.
MAKES: $1/2$ cup (125 ml)

ASIAN PEANUT SAUCE

¼ cup (60 g) crunchy peanut butter
1 tablespoon soft brown sugar
1 tablespoon soy sauce
1 clove garlic, crushed
½ teaspoon sambal oelek
3 teaspoons fresh lime juice

Put all of the ingredients, except the lime juice, in a small saucepan over low heat. Add ⅓ cup (80 ml) water and stir until the mixture is smooth. Remove from the heat and stir in the lime juice until well combined. Taste and add some sambal oelek or lime if desired. Use immediately or store in an airtight container for up to 2-3 days. You can use this peanut sauce to serve alongside chicken skewers or as a substitute for any satay sauce.
MAKES: ⅔ cup (150 ml)

VARIATIONS

● Add finely chopped lemongrass and/or grated fresh ginger for additional flavour. For a creamier satay sauce add 2 tablespoons low-fat coconut milk or yogurt just before removing from the heat.

SWEET CHILLI NOODLES

250 g (8 oz) wok-ready thin Chinese egg noodles
1 tablespoon sunflower oil
2 cloves garlic, sliced
1 tablespoon grated fresh ginger
1¼ cups (125 g) sliced snow peas (mangetout)
6 spring onions (scallions), finely chopped
¼ cup (60 ml) sweet chilli sauce
2 tablespoons salt-reduced soy sauce

Cook the noodles according to the packet instructions. Drain well and set aside until needed. Heat the sunflower oil in a wok or large non-stick frying pan over high heat and cook the garlic and ginger for 30 seconds. Add the snow peas and spring onion and stir-fry for 1 minute, then add the noodles, sweet chilli sauce and soy sauce and cook for 1-2 minutes to heat through, tossing to coat in the sauce. Serve the warm noodle mixture with Teriyaki swordfish skewers (see page 183).
SERVES: 4

STIR-FRY NOODLES

400 g (14 oz) wok-ready hokkien (egg) noodles
1 teaspoon sesame oil
1 tablespoon sunflower oil
2 cups (180 g) bean sprouts, trimmed
1 onion, thinly sliced
1 tablespoon salt-reduced soy sauce
2 tablespoons chopped fresh coriander (cilantro) leaves

Cook the noodles according to the packet instructions. Drain well, return to the pan and drizzle over the sesame oil; set aside until needed. Meanwhile, heat the sunflower oil in a wok or large non-stick frying pan over medium-high heat. Add the bean sprouts and onion and stir-fry for about 2 minutes, then add the noodles and stir-fry for 3 minutes, tossing well to combine. Pour the soy sauce over the noodle mixture and sprinkle with the coriander. Serve with Tamarind vegetables and cashews (see page 230).
SERVES: 4

QUICK NOODLES

1 tablespoon sunflower oil
½ cup (90 g) fresh or canned baby corn
1 red capsicum (bell pepper), halved, seeded and sliced
1 clove garlic, crushed
2 cups (500 ml) salt-reduced vegetable stock
225 g (8 oz) dried thin egg noodles
1⅓ cups (100 g) shredded bok choy

Heat the sunflower oil in a wok or large non-stick frying pan over medium heat. Add the baby corn and capsicum and stir-fry for 2-3 minutes, or until starting to soften. Add the garlic and stir-fry for 30 seconds, then add the vegetable stock and noodles. Cover and cook for 2 minutes, or until the noodles have softened, then stir in the bok choy. Cook for 1 minute more, or until all of the stock has been absorbed and the vegetables are tender. Serve with Sesame seafood stir-fry (see page 198).
SERVES: 4

THAI SALAD DRESSING

1 tablespoon peanut or sunflower oil
2 long red chillies, seeded and finely chopped
1 tablespoon grated fresh ginger
1 stem lemongrass, white part only, finely chopped
2 cloves garlic, finely chopped
1/4 cup (60 ml) fresh lime juice
1 tablespoon fish sauce
1 teaspoon soft brown sugar

Heat the peanut oil in a large non-stick frying pan over medium heat. Add the chilli, ginger, lemongrass and garlic and stir-fry for 1 minute. Remove from the heat and allow to cool slightly. In a small bowl, combine the lime juice, fish sauce and sugar. Add the chilli mixture and stir until well combined. Use immediately, drizzled over salad leaves or try a combination of sliced green mango, shredded coconut, bean sprouts, fresh coriander (cilantro) leaves and chopped peanuts.
MAKES: 1/3 cup (80 ml)

GREEN CURRY PASTE

4 French shallots (eschalots), chopped
1 teaspoon shrimp or anchovy paste
3 cloves garlic, chopped
2 dried kaffir lime (makrut) leaves, crushed, or
    1 teaspoon finely grated lime zest
10 cm (4 inch) stem lemongrass, inner stem chopped
1 tablespoon coriander seeds
1 tablespoon grated fresh ginger
1 teaspoon freshly grated nutmeg
1 teaspoon cumin seeds
1 teaspoon white peppercorns
6 long green chillies, seeded and sliced
1/4 cup (60 ml) low-fat coconut cream

Put all of the ingredients in a food processor or blender and process until smooth and combined. Use the curry paste immediately or place in an airtight container, cover with vegetable oil and store in the refrigerator for up to 4 days. Alternatively, pack the paste into an ice-cube tray, freeze, pop out the paste cubes and store in a self-sealing, freezer-safe plastic bag in the freezer.
MAKES: 3/4 cup (185 g)

RED CURRY PASTE

1 tablespoon coriander seeds
3-6 long red chillies, trimmed
    of stems
4 French shallots (eschalots),
    chopped
1 red onion, chopped
4 cloves garlic, chopped
10 cm (4 inch) stem lemongrass,
    inner stem chopped
1/4 cup (10 g) fresh coriander
    (cilantro) leaves
2 kaffir lime (makrut) leaves or
    finely grated zest of 2 limes
1 teaspoon freshly grated nutmeg
1 teaspoon cumin seeds
1 teaspoon white peppercorns
2 teaspoons shrimp or anchovy paste

Toast the coriander seeds in a frying pan over medium-high heat for about 30 seconds. Transfer to a food processor or blender and add the chillies, shallots, onion, garlic, lemongrass, coriander, kaffir lime leaves, zest, nutmeg, cumin seeds and white peppercorns. Process until all the ingredients are well combined. Dry-roast the shrimp paste in a frying pan over medium heat for 2-3 minutes, stirring constantly. Add to the chilli mixture and process until smooth. Use the paste at once, or place in an airtight container, cover with vegetable oil and store in the refrigerator for up to 2 weeks.
MAKES: 1 cup (185 g)

SOY AND SESAME MARINADE

1/4 cup (60 ml) fresh lemon juice
1/2 teaspoon salt
2 tablespoons sesame oil
1 large clove garlic, crushed
1 tablespoon salt-reduced soy sauce

Put all of the ingredients in a small, non-metallic bowl and stir until well combined. Pour the marinade into a self-sealing bag and add the seafood, meat or poultry that you wish to marinate. Place the bag in the refrigerator for at least 1 hour before cooking.
MAKES: 1/2 cup (125 ml)

CHILLI JAM

250 g (8 oz) capsicums (bell peppers), halved and
     seeded
2 long red chillies, seeded and roughly chopped
1/4 cup (60 ml) olive oil
1 small onion, finely chopped
2 cloves garlic, finely chopped
1 tablespoon grated palm sugar (jaggery)
1 tablespoon fish sauce
2 teaspoons tamarind paste
1 tablespoon chopped fresh coriander (cilantro)
     leaves
1 tablespoon chopped fresh mint

Preheat a grill (broiler) to high. Place the capsicum
under the hot grill, skin side up, and cook for about
10 minutes, or until the skins have blistered and
blackened. Transfer the hot capsicums to a large
heatproof bowl, cover with plastic wrap and cool
or about 10 minutes, or until safe to handle. Peel
off the skins, then roughly chop the flesh. Transfer
to a food processor, add the chilli and process to
make a smooth purée. Meanwhile, heat the olive
oil in a small saucepan over medium heat. Add the
onion and cook for 1–2 minutes, or until softened.
Add the garlic and cook for 30 seconds, then add
the capsicum purée, palm sugar, fish sauce and
tamarind paste. Continue to simmer for 10 minutes
over low heat, stirring occasionally. Remove from
the heat and stir through the coriander and mint;
allow to cool to room temperature. Use immediately
as a dip with any of your favourite starters, mix
into noodle dishes or serve as a condiment with
your favourite beef or chicken stir-fry and rice.
Chilli jam can be stored in an airtight container
in the refrigerator for up to 2 weeks.
MAKES: 1 cup (250 g)

STEAMED OR BOILED RICE

1 cup (200 g) white long-grain rice

Put the rice in a bowl, place under cold running
water and use your fingers to toss the rice and rinse
off any dust or dirt. Drain in a colander – the water
should run clear. To steam the rice, prick a few holes
in a sheet of baking (parchment) paper and use it to
line the base of a steamer. Place a layer of cheese-
cloth, or muslin, over the top, then spread the rice in
an even layer inside. Cover with a lid and place the
steamer over a wok of simmering water for about
40 minutes, or until the rice is tender. To boil the
rice, put the rice in a heavy-based saucepan with
1²/₃ cups (425 ml) water. Bring to the boil, then
reduce the heat to low and simmer for about
15 minutes, or until the water has been absorbed
and the rice is tender. Fluff the rice with a fork
before serving.
SERVES: 4

MERMAID'S TRESSES

350 g (12 oz) bok choy
peanut oil, for deep-frying
caster (superfine) sugar, to taste

Finely shred the bok choy and dry with paper towel
to remove any excess moisture. Fill a wok or large
saucepan with enough oil to come about one-third
of the way up the saucepan. You will need to heat
the oil so that it is very hot – when you drop a small
amount of the bok choy into the oil it should sizzle
immediately. Deep-fry the bok choy, in batches, for
about 20 seconds each, or until the leaves have
shrivelled and darkened, being careful that they do
not burn. Drain well on paper towels and repeat until
all of the bok choy is cooked. Sprinkle with a little
salt and sugar, to taste, and serve as a snack or use
a little as a garnish over vegetable or rice dishes.
SERVES: 4

VARIATIONS
● You can also use choy sum (Chinese flowering
cabbage) or gai larn (Chinese cabbage) if bok choy
is unavailable. Both are available from Asian grocery
stores or most large supermarkets.

Index

Index

WEIGHTS AND MEASURES

Australian metric cup and spoon measurements have been used throughout this book: 1 cup = 250 ml; 1 tablespoon = 20 ml and 1 teaspoon = 5 ml. If using the smaller imperial cup and spoon measures (where 1 cup = 235 ml and 1 tablespoon = 15 ml), some adjustments may need to be made. A small variation in the weight or volume of most ingredients is unlikely to adversely affect a recipe. All cup and spoon measures are level, unless stated otherwise. Ingredients are generally listed by their weight or volume with cup measurements given for convenience, unless the conversion is imperfect, whereby the ingredients are listed by weight or volume only.

Sometimes conversions within a recipe are not exact but are the closest conversion that is a suitable measurement for each system. Use either the metric or the imperial measurements; do not mix the two systems. Can sizes vary between countries and manufacturers; if the stated size is unavailable, use the nearest equivalent.

NUTRITIONAL ANALYSIS

Each recipe is accompanied by a nutrient profile showing kilojoules (kJ), calories (kcal), protein, fat (including saturated fat), carbohydrate (including sugars), fibre. and sodium. Serving suggestions, garnishes and optional ingredients are not included in the nutritional analysis. For the recipe analysis we used FoodWorks ® based on Australian and New Zealand food composition data. In line with current nutritional recommendations, use salt-reduced stock and soy sauce wherever possible.

ALTERNATIVE TERMS AND SUBSTITUTES

capsicum - sweet pepper, bell pepper
Chinese five spice - five spice powder
coriander - cilantro
corn cob - mealie/miele
crisp fried noodles - 2-minute noodles (do not use the sachet)
cumquat - kumquat
eggplant - aubergine, brinjal
English spinach - baby spinach; not the heavily veined, thick-leafed vegetable sold as spinach or silver beet
filo - phyllo
fish substitutes - for blue-eyed cod, bream, ling, snapper, flathead, use any firm white-fleshed fish such as cod, hake or kabeljou
fresh shiitake mushrooms - rehydrated dried shiitake mushrooms
hokkien noodles - 2-minute noodles or other fast-cooking noodle
kebab - kebob, skewer

kepak manis - sweet soy sauce
Lebanese cucumber - Mediterranean cucumber, short cucumber
oregano - oreganum
papaya - pawpaw
passionfruit - granadilla
pot stickers - Chinese dumplings
rockmelon - spanspek, cantaloupe
silver beet - Swiss chard, often sold as spinach in South Africa
Swiss brown mushrooms - brown mushrooms
telegraph cucumber - English cucumber, long cucumber
vanilla extract - vanilla essence
Vietnamese mint - mint or combination of cilantro and mint
wholemeal - wholewheat
witlof - witloof, Belgian endive
zucchini - baby marrow, courgette

Copyright 2011 The Reader's Digest Association, Inc.
Copyright © Reader's Digest (Australia) Pty Limited 2011
Copyright © Reader's Digest Association Far East Limited 2011
Philippines Copyright © Reader's Digest Association Far East
Limited 2011

Library of Congress Cataloging-in-Publication Data available
upon request.

ISBN 978-1-60652-350-6

We are committed to both the quality of our products and the service
we provide to our customers. We value your comments,
so please feel free to contact us:

The Reader's Digest Association, Inc.,
Adult Trade Publishing
44 S. Broadway
White Plains, NY 10601

For more Reader's Digest products and information,
visit our website:
www.rd.com (in the United States)
www.readersdigest.ca (in Canada)

Low Fat No Fat Asian Cooking contains some material first published in
the following Reader's Digest books: *30 Minute Cookbook; Beat High
Blood Pressure Cookbook; Cook Smart for a Healthy Heart, Cut Your
Cholesterol: Diabetes Cookbook; Eat Well Stay Well; Everyday Arthritis
Solutions; Good Food for Less; Healthy One-Dish Cooking; Looking After
Your Body; Midweek Meals Made Easy; Super Salads; The Great Potato
Cookbook; Vegetables for Vitality.*

Text Brigid Treloar (pp 8-17)
Project Editor Jacqueline Blanchard
Designer Michelle Cutler
Senior Designer Donna Heldon
Nutritional Analysis Toni Gumley
Proofreader Susan McCreery
Indexer Diane Harriman
Senior Production Controller Monique Tesoriero
Editorial Project Manager General Books Deborah Nixon

READER'S DIGEST GENERAL BOOKS
Editorial Director Elaine Russell
Managing Editor Rosemary McDonald
Art Director Carole Orbell

CREDITS
Pages 21, 29, 41, 61, 79, 81, 109, 119, 125, 159, 171, 205, 217, 236:
Photographer Stuart Scott, **Stylist** Trish Heagerty,
Food preparation Wendy Quisumbing, **Recipes** Brigid Treloar

All images except the following are owned by Reader's Digest:
Dreamstime 15 t; iStockphoto 15 b, 17 c; Shutterstock 4-5, 6, 9,
10 l, 10 c, 11 c, 12-13, 14, 15 ct, 15 cb, 17 t, 17 b

Front cover: Low-fat laksa, page 40
Back cover: *from top to bottom* Kung pao chicken, page 78;
Chicken lemongrass skewers, page 81; Singapore noodles, page 60;
Pleated seafood dumplings, page 22

Page 2: *clockwise from top left* Singapore noodles, page 60;
Hand-rolled sushi, page 20; Chilli crab, page 204; Chicken
lemongrass skewers, page 81

Prepress by Sinnott Bros, Sydney
Printed and bound by Leo Paper Products, China

1 3 5 7 9 10 8 6 4 2